Votes for Cricket

Votes for Cricket

The Story of Westminster Politicians Who Played First-Class Cricket

by David Lemmon with Douglas Smith

The Breedon Books
Publishing Company
Derby

First published in Great Britain by
The Breedon Books Publishing Company Limited
Breedon House, 44 Friar Gate, Derby, DE1 1DA.
2000

ISBN 1 85983 188 5

Printed and bound by Butler & Tanner Ltd., Selwood Printing Works, Caxton Road, Frome, Somerset.

Colour separations and jacket printing by
GreenShires Group Ltd, Leicester.

Contents

Foreword

by Douglas Smith

CRICKET'S contribution to the wider world has frequently been exulted – namely its opportunity for higher individual performances within a competitive team framework. Victorians described this in poetic, even quasi religious terms, yet it applies equally today, although perhaps with less of the romance and more of the hostility.

Not surprising, therefore, one sees personal styles displayed on the field of play translating themselves on a wider stage – sometimes successfully, often not. Political pitches, for example, can be very different. Sir Stanley Jackson is on paper the best all-rounder in both spheres. One of the most effective cricketing performers, particularly in a crisis, he was, however, far less influential in his various party posts.

As this book shows by looking at those who played first-class cricket as well as being members of the UK Parliament, 'Jacker's' experience was not unique. Principally, of course, incompatibility lies in the reverse direction. Many skilled politicians were only occasional top-class cricketers. Pressure of time is the main culprit. Alfred Lyttelton could, one suspects, have achieved almost anything on the broader scene – as he did so much in several sports – but there were not enough hours in his day. Generally speaking the Lords has been a happier second home for cricketers, precisely because of its less demanding requirements.

Time is not, of course, the only factor. Cunning is a useful cricketing skill, as 'WG' demonstrated, but it palls by comparison with what is seen in the Westminster and Whitehall world, where such umpires as exist are usually unsighted.

A personal recollection, albeit at lowly level, reveals this distinction. When I first ventured on to the political scene in the early 1960s, it was made clear that one of my tasks was to ensure closer co-operation between the Tory Party in Parliament and its agents in the field – at that time more numerous and not without a certain power if they chose to exert it. "We must have greater goodwill between the Officers and Sergeants," was the injunction, delivered by none other than the then Party chairman, R. A. Butler. So, when invited to play for the Agents X1 against Conservative MPs (matches which figure in Lords and Commons Cricket records), I scented an opportunity for rapid personal advancement.

Picture the scene. Hurlingham Club on a splendid July afternoon. Ladies in large hats; ambitious young bucks in loud blazers; cloth-eared dogs barking; magnums of champagne. Naturally the politicians bat first. Two dignified and beaming old buffers emerge as the openers – Sir Walter Bromley-Davenport and Sir Charles Mott-Radclyffe no less. For what seems so clearly a social occasion, I begin to mark out a modest run-up.

Turning to discuss field placing with my captain, it is apparent there are hidden undercurrents. The previous year's fixture had, I later learned, suffered from some dodgy decisions (one umpire being in search of a safe seat) and a delayed declaration. By Jardine out of Larwood was a good description of the field he had already set – four short legs; three slips; wicketkeeper nearly hard against the sight screen. "I hear you're quick, Smudger," snarled the skipper. "Now's the time to prove it." It was an order which seemed somewhat at variance with the mission statement given only a few days earlier by RAB.

A time for rapid thinking. Causing by-elections seemed an unwise early career move. By bowling at fullish length, wickets fell swiftly enough to satisfy the agents' bloodlust and a comfortable victory after early tea. A lesson in the importance of research was duly learned. I have never discovered whether my five wickets, all being double-barrelled MPs, constituted a ten-wicket haul.

Lords and Commons Cricket does not much concern us henceforth, although several of those included (but, typically, not 'Jacker') played their parts on that amateur stage. One recalls Aidan Crawley, then well into his 60s, huffing and puffing his way through some opening overs when he discovered his XI had only two bowlers, both of them slow. Needless to say his 'wobblers' produced three wickets. Also there was cultured batting by Sir Nicholas Scott and David (now Lord) Gibson-Watt to show how easily both could have graced the first-class game. Lord Orr-Ewing's compilation of articles in *A Celebration of 140 years of Lords and Commons Cricket* in 1988 can be recommended as a book to give the full flavour.

Throughout research for our book we were constantly struck by the 'might have beens' – hence David Lemmon's decision to have a 'Twelfth Man' section for those who nearly qualified. It could so easily have been more lengthy. When a full-scale creation of new peers was being considered to resolve the 1910 constitutional crisis, the names of W. G. Grace and Prince Ranjitsinhji were apparently on the list, as was C. B. Fry. But we could not resist writing of Charles Fry (who can?) in any event since he also came within 200 votes of inclusion under his own steam. More recently, of course, one must give Lord MacLaurin an honourable mention. As a skilful young cricketer, he could well have played some first-class games if supermarketing had not claimed him. Now, as chairman of the England and Wales Cricket Board, he is helping to reshape the game as powerfully as anyone in these pages. May he be successful. The need has rarely been so great.

A different problem of selection had to be faced with earlier chapters. First-class matches are not easily identified until one reaches the 1860s. Previous games are often a matter of personal judgement. A simple example are the earlier Oxford v Cambridge matches when it seems if the Hon Treasurer chose to play, he duly did, and collected his blue, regardless of skill or current form. Later we have the Europeans, who played top-level cricket in imperial India. Details of their players who were also Parliamentarians are hard to find. One suspects they number more than the single MP, Jackie Smyth, who we report here.

No doubt, despite our best efforts, there will be corrections to be made. Cheerful assistance in proposing them for further editions will be welcomed. For those who nitpick needlessly – and some such haunt the cricket world – there will be a less friendly reception, as David and I resolved from the first. They will be met by the reply Brian Luckhurst gave when it was retrospectively – and bizarrely – resolved that England's 1970 series against the Rest of the World could not have Test status. Having battled to a not-out century against McKenzie, Barlow, Proctor, Sobers, Intikhab and Gibbs, thereby winning the match, his response to the later suggestion that he might need to return his England cap was... well, perhaps better left unspecific. *Corinthians 3; 5* puts it more properly: 'For the letter killeth, but the spirit giveth life.'

Restricting the number of tall tales and short stories was a real problem we encountered. They are a sparkling skein which runs through most of the games literature, intentionally or not. It is all too easy to fall into anecdotage.

A few examples are, however, irresistible. The on-close inspection less than saintly Sir Pelham Warner recounts in his autobiography *Long Innings* of how Lord Hawke handled his professionals. Born in Lincolnshire, he had a proper objectivity on how to stimulate Yorkshiremen. He devised a running 'marks' system for payment by results. Hence Sir Pelham hearing Hawke say, as he departed caught splendidly by Tunnicliffe at slip: "Ten shillings for that one, John."

Lord Lionel Tennyson, who features later, retained the Hampshire wicketkeeper, Walter Livsey, as his supernumerary in the winter months. Accordingly they knew each other well. One gloomy evening Livsey arrived at the wicket where Tennyson felt stumps should be pulled for the day. Time for a broad hint to the umpires. "What do you think about the light, Livsey?" he boomed. Came the reply: "I can hear you, milord, but I can't see you."

Willy Rees-Davies, whose cricketing career we also chart, was a steady source of stories during his long House of Commons stint. Over an early evening drink in the Strangers' Bar he mentioned that he once had Bradman dropped in the slips at 1 and then he went on to a century. Dubious glances all round at this recollection but later that evening at his home he showed me the scorecard for the 1938 Cambridge v Australian tourists match. A massive Aussie total – Bradman with 137 of it and Rees-Davies with 2 for 214 off 43 overs. "Turn it over", said Willy. There on the back, in the Don's distinctive handwriting, were the words: 'I acknowledge I was dropped off the bowling of Mr Rees-Davies at the start of the innings.' An example of gall and prescience entirely typical of the man – Rees-Davies, I mean, not The Don!

British Prime Ministers especially have often loved cricket as much – and often more – than the pressures of noble office. Clement Attlee was a man of few words but more fluent when his real interests were affected. His Press Officer (spin in those days was confined to cricket) persuaded Attlee to install a news ticker tape at No 10 because it carried the county scores. The Prime Minister was once heard openly muttering as he studied it: "What's all this political stuff doing on my cricket machine."

Sir Alec Douglas-Home knew his history. Talking of the remarkable Lyttelton family, he reflected that even Canon Edward Lyttelton of St Paul's could not walk down its nave without wondering whether it would take spin.

Sir Edward Heath is, of course, a Man of Kent and keenly follows the county's progress. Speaking at the KCCC 100th Anniversary Dinner in 1970 he forecast a General Election that same year with himself as the winner and hoped Kent would be equally successful. In mid-June, against majority judgements, so it turned out to be. Kent at the time were very bottom of the County Championship. Came a telegram from the new Prime Minister to the effect: "I've done my bit, what about you?" By early September Colin Cowdrey was captain of the Championship side.

Finally we have the recent example of John Major who, having lost the 1997 General Election, duly delivered his resignation seals to Her Majesty the Queen. Where did he go from Buckingham Palace? Straight to The Oval, of course, to see Surrey in action.

As we shall further note, a few political predecessors would have been applauding this, his last Prime Ministerial decision.

March 2000

Photographic Acknowledgements
Photographs have been supplied by Popperfoto and the MCC Archive.

Pioneers

THE Universities of Oxford and Cambridge first met on the cricket field in 1827. The weather was bad, and after each side had completed an innings apiece, the match was postponed for a week. In fact, it never resumed, and the two teams did not meet again for another two years. It was not until 1838, the fourth game between the universities, that the match became an annual event.

This fourth match was rather a sad affair. G. A. Seymour, who had been a leading batsman at Eton three years earlier and who was up at King's College, Cambridge, died suddenly shortly before the game, and his death robbed Cambridge not only of his talent but of the services of several of their leading players who were mourning his loss. The weakened Cambridge side was bowled out for 57 and 47 and was beaten by 98 runs. Opening the innings for Cambridge were W. Massey and the Fourth Baron Lyttelton.

Lyttelton was bowled by Lowth for 0 in the first innings, and run out for 0 in the second. This was the extent of his career in important cricket matches although his name was to appear in a team of Worcestershire gentlemen who took on Clarke's All England XI in 1851.

Such a record was unlikely to give Lord Lyttelton a permanent place in the annals of cricket, but he is most renowned as being the father of eight sons, six of whom played the game at first-class level. Only the seven Walkers of Southgate can challenge this achievement, but their sire must bow to Lyttelton in other areas.

In January 1846, the Fourth Baron Lyttelton was appointed to serve in Sir Robert Peel's government as Under Secretary to the War and Colonial Offices. In itself, this appointment had little political significance, but, in cricketing terms, it was historic, for Lyttelton was the first man to have appeared in an important match and to have been elevated to hold government office.

Unfortunately, Lyttelton's political career was scarcely longer than his career in major cricket had been. Within six months, Peel's great administration had come to an end, and Lord John Russell and the Whigs came to power. It was to be another 28 years before a first-class cricketer was to hold government office.

Of course, Lyttelton was not the first statesman to display a passion for cricket. The game was an accepted pursuit for a gentleman, as Lord Chesterfield reminded his son in one of those innumerable letters. In the 18th century, the Bare Knuckle days of the game, men of political influence and stature were prominent in the growth and advance of cricket, and none was to have a greater influence than Charles Lennox, Earl March, Second Duke of Richmond. His biographer, John Marshall, was to describe him as 'the Duke who was Cricket'.

A grandson of Charles II, Lennox was a patron of the opera, a generous host who entertained beyond his means, and a devoted husband to a wife of exceptional beauty. He was a soldier and a practical joker who, during his career, was Mayor of Chichester, a Lord Justice, a Privy Councillor and Master of Horse at the Court of George II. In this last role, he had the unenviable task of acting as a liaison between the King and the Prince of Wales when the two had become estranged.

While, as Earl March, he was on the grand tour of Europe, his friends fought for his election as Member of Parliament for Chichester, the constituency in which his Goodwood home was situated. 'His devoted friends,' writes Marshall, 'had to strive and to bribe mightily and even drink deeply, to secure this distinction.' An old retainer on the estate practically worked himself to death on behalf of his master, and Richmond's sister Anne told him in a letter: 'Lord William and George Macarthy take as much pains, for they are forst to drink strong bear and smoak with all the voaters twis a week which you may gus is not very agreeable to them, and I believe would not do it for aney body but you.'

One cannot conceive of a candidate today daring to absent himself during the campaign from the constituency he was contesting, but Richmond repaid the debt in kind some years later when he helped his uncle, Jeremy Brudenell, win the Chichester seat in the West Sussex elections.

Although he was a Whig, Richmond was less successful in winning advantages for his friends from the Prime Minister (not a title he used) Sir Robert Walpole, 'the first great House of Commons man in British history', and the first chief minister to live at No 10 Downing Street.

The failure of Richmond's persuasive powers to influence the chief minister were, no doubt, due as much to his own lack of political acumen as to Walpole's renowned integrity and resolution. Richmond's main political achievement was that he was grandfather to one of Britain's most eminent statesmen.

His eldest child, Lady Caroline Lennox, was courted by Henry Fox, MP for Windsor, and a Lord of the Treasury. He was reputed to be a ruthless and cunning politician, a man of humble origins and doubtful reputation. When he asked the duke for Lady Caroline's hand in marriage he was most emphatically refused. The thwarted lovers responded by eloping, and, eventually, they were reconciled with the Duke and Duchess. In 1749, Caroline gave birth to a son, Charles James Fox, who was to become a far more distinguished politician than either his father or grandfather.

Richmond's main interests lay outside politics and the affairs of state. At Goodwood, he planted more than 1,000 Cedars of Lebanon, and he introduced a variety of wild and exotic animals on to his estate.

He enjoyed riding to hounds, but his greatest passion was cricket. It is likely that his enthusiasm for the game exceeded his talent, but his contribution to its development in Sussex and its growth elsewhere was immense.

On his estate at Goodwood, he employed men who were renowned at cricket. They were given tasks as coachmen or gardeners, but, in fact, they were one of the earliest bodies of professional cricketers, and they made his sides among the strongest in the land. He gave patronage to the village side of Slindon, and they became to Sussex what Hambledon were to become to Hampshire.

In July 1727, in conjunction with A. Brodrick of Pepperharowe, he agreed a covenant of 16 clauses to govern play in two matches the two men had arranged between their respective sides. These articles of agreement were, in effect, one of the earliest sets of laws of the game, and it is worth noting that Richmond's fellow signatory to the agreement, Alan Brodrick, whose estate was in Surrey, had a political background that was stronger than the Duke's. His father had been MP for Cork and was successively Solicitor General and Attorney-General for Ireland, and Speaker in the Irish House of Commons. On moving to Surrey, he was elected MP for Midhurst. Brodrick himself, later Viscount Middleton, followed a career which saw him become Commissioner of the Customs and Joint Comptroller of the Army accounts.

Nearly a century later, Lord John Russell was to warn of the evil results of 'mixing politics with religion'. On the results of combining politics with cricket, he gave no guidance, but by the end of the 18th century, any warning would have been in vain. The two were inextricably blended.

Cricket had entered into the soul of the Lennox family. The Third Duke of Richmond captained Sussex against Hambledon, and his nephew, the Fourth Duke, was to become the greatest cricketer of this distinguished line.

Charles Lennox was born in 1764. He was one of those natural talents that excel at all sports to which they turn their hand. He was the supreme athlete. He ran, and he jumped, and, above all, he played cricket, being an outstanding batsman and wicketkeeper for two decades.

He was a military man who rose to the rank of general, and he played cricket wherever the army took him. In 1786, he is seen playing for the White Conduit Club against Kent and opening the innings with Lord Winchilsea. In the following years, he appeared for Kent, for Surrey, for Sir Horace Mann's sides and a variety of other teams. He batted high in the order, often opening, and scored consistently in an age when runs were harder to come by than they are today.

Lennox's relationship with Lord Winchilsea extended beyond that of opening partners. Both were army men and both were concerned about the future of the White Conduit Club. This had replaced the London Club as the fashionable cricket club for the noblemen, but there was growing concern about the unenclosed ground at Islington where the Club played and practised. The noblemen often found themselves the victims of public abuse.

This discontent spread, and, in 1786, Lennox and Winchilsea approached one of the general attendants and ground bowlers and asked him if he would care to establish a private ground. They assured him that he would have the full support of the Club if he undertook the venture. He readily agreed. His name was Thomas Lord.

Lord set up his new ground in what is now Dorset Square, and the Marylebone Cricket Club came into existence in 1787, with Charles Lennox as one of its founder members. The new club played its first game on Lord's new ground the following year. It was against fellow members of the White Conduit Club which, thereafter, ceased to exist. Lennox was unable to play in this match, but he was never far from cricket, nor was he ever far from action of some kind.

In 1789, he was appointed to the command of a battalion of the Coldstream Guards. The Colonel of the regiment, Frederick, Duke of York, brother of King George III, was reported to have made remarks which Lennox found insulting. The two men fought a duel on Wimbledon Common, but, although a shot was fired, neither the Duke nor the Colonel was injured. It was agreed that honour had been satisfied, and the Duke of York was entertained at Lennox's home some time later.

Lennox was posted to Scotland, but not before he had time to fight another duel, this time with a pamphleteer, Theophilus Swift, who had made a scurrilous attack on him. Lennox wounded Swift, but the satirist survived.

In Edinburgh, Lennox arranged cricket matches, as he did wherever he served, including the Caribbean where he played in the Leeward Islands.

In 1806, he became the Fourth Duke of Richmond, and, a year later, he was appointed Lord Lieutenant of Ireland where, not unnaturally, he played as much cricket as possible.

It was then that interest centred on Richmond as a politician. The same year in which he had succeeded to his title saw the death of William Pitt the Younger. At a time of national concern, Pitt's death created something of a void in politics. A ministry of all talents to suit all factions was possible, but the debate concerned who was to lead such a ministry. Reluctantly, George III was forced to accept the return from the wilderness of Charles James Fox, Richmond's cousin, and Fox was named as chief minister. Fox was a sick man, and within the year, he, too, was dead, and was succeeded by Lord Portland.

Men of stature like Walpole, Pitt and Fox had led England in the 18th century, but now came a time of makeshift ministries. Portland died in 1809. Who should succeed him as chief minister? The Fourth Duke of Richmond was one of those who came under serious consideration, but the selection lighted on Spencer Perceval who was to carve himself a unique place in the history books. Richmond's chance was gone, and it was to be 154 years and 31 prime ministers later before a first-class cricketer was to occupy No 10 Downing Street.

Undeterred and untroubled, Charles Lennox, Duke of Richmond continued with his illustrious military career and his highly active life. In the days before Waterloo, he was quartered near Brussels, and he organised a cricket match between teams of officers of the Brigade of Guards.

From the cricket match, the officers strolled to the famous and spectacular ball which was given at Quatre Bras on 15 June 1815. This 'Eve of Waterloo Ball', as it was later termed, was hosted by the Duchess of Richmond who had borne Lennox 14 children.

The Duke fought alongside Wellington at Waterloo, and one of his sons, Lord March, was with him in that historic engagement. Like Wellington, both escaped unharmed from that 'damned close run thing', and the Duke of Richmond became Governor-General of Canada.

Richmond certainly did not introduce cricket to Canada, for it had long been popular there among British garrisons, but he did help to cement its popularity and was noted for arranging cricket matches on the Heights of Abraham. This was to be his last great cricketing achievement for it was in Canada that he met his death.

In the breadth of his talent and the scope of his achievement, this man of remarkable energy anticipated Alfred Lyttelton, Charles Fry and Stanley Jackson, yet, in the midst of his outstanding courage and unrelenting confidence, he often confessed to a dread of hydrophobia. It was a prophetic fear. In 1819, he was bitten by what is sometimes referred to as a tame fox, and sometimes as a pet dog. The animal was rabid, and Charles Lennox, Duke of Richmond, died painfully of hydrophobia. He was 55 years old. Few men have packed so much into so short a time.

The description of an earlier Charles Lennox as 'the Duke who was cricket' leads us to another giant of the game, George Osbaldeston. Once famously described as the 'Squire of England', he was as commanding an all-round figure as the Fourth Duke.

Born in 1787, Osbaldeston was educated at Eton and Brasenose, where he became master of his first pack of hounds as an undergraduate. This was only the start of a famous hunting career. Small wonder he quitted without a degree, given his other sporting pursuits. Inevitably a keen steeplechaser, he was also expert with a shotgun (98 pheasants from 100 shots) and a master fisherman as well.

Only 5ft 6ins in height, Osbaldeston was vast chested and a powerful pugilist when the need arose – which, given his short temper and fierce pride, it occasionally did. The Squire was, of course, a great gambler in line with the spirit of the times. At the age of 44 he took a wager that he could cover 200 miles in ten hours. Using a fresh horse every four miles he duly did so – at an average of 26mph, with 78 minutes to spare.

One of the most famous cricketing wagers featured Osbaldeston and another larger than life figure of the period, the Revd Lord Frederick Beauclerk, fourth son of the Fifth Duke of St Albans and accordingly a descendant of Charles II and Nell Gwynn. In 1831 the pair had fought a duel at Wormwood Scrubs, both bullets happily missing their targets, but Osbaldeston's single-wicket match challenge to Beauclerk aroused still more public interest. For a stake of 50 guineas he and the well-known professional William Lambert took on Beauclerk and his professional, one T. C. Howard.

Just prior to the encounter the Squire fell ill and sought a postponement. His Lordship responded simply: "Play or pay." So Osbaldeston made a token appearance, leaving Lambert to tackle the two opponents single-handed. He proved well up to the task, scoring 80 in two innings and dismissing the rival pair twice for a total of 66. Knowing Beauclerk's fiery temperament well, the professional bowled him a long series of wides (which did not then count against the score) suddenly to insert a swift, straight ball. One is only surprised that another duel did not ensue.

Osbaldeston represented East Retford as a Liberal from 1812-18. He declared he 'did not care' for Parliament and therefore devoted his time to cricket as one of the fastest underarm bowlers and powerful hitters of the day. He died at 80 in his home close to Lord's, sadly excluded by his foes from renewing the MCC membership he had earlier resigned. Beauclerk was unforgiving and not immodest either, once claiming of himself:

"I am the batsman and the bat,
I am the bowler and the ball,
The umpire, the pavilion cat,
The roller, pitch and stumps and all."

Whether such an approach would have succeeded with electors was never put to the test.

We now hark back. Charles Lennox had played some of his earliest cricket alongside Sir Horatio Mann and for Mann's XI, for, like Lennox, he was a member of the White Conduit Club and one of those who had prompted and encouraged Thomas Lord to establish his new enclosed ground.

Mann was 19 years Lennox's senior so that he was already a veteran when the future Duke of Richmond took the stage. Indeed, the records of Mann's career are, in the main part, lost. He was educated at Charterhouse and at Cambridge, but he was never one to let academic pursuits interfere with his lust for life. He was a Man of Kent, owning houses in at least ten parishes in the county. Surprisingly, he only rented the two at which he presented most of his cricket, at Bourne Park and at Dandelion Paddock, near Margate. He was the first great patron of Kent cricket, responsible for early endeavours to form a county club.

There is no record of his playing days before 1768, and the last recorded match in which he played was in 1782 when he made 0 and 1 against Hampshire at Moulsey Hurst. At Bourne, in 1773, he was one of the four gentlemen in the Kent side that took on Surrey and lost by 153 runs. Surrey's enormous victory was celebrated in verse by the Revd John Duncombe whose *Surrey Triumphant or the Kentishmen's Defeat* was a parody of *Chevy Chase*. Horace Mann is described as 'a batter of great might', and his 22 in the second innings was the second highest score in a total of 78. Duncombe enthused:

'He swung till both his arms did ache
His bat of seasoned wood,
Till down his azure sleeves the sweat
Ran trickling like a flood.'

As we have said, many records have been lost, and this innings of 22 is his highest noted score that we have, but it is as a patron, a sponsor that he is best remembered.

He was a wonderful friend to cricket in Kent, and for the best part of 30 years he was responsible for scores of matches, many of them ones involving the county. There were reports of crowds of 15,000-20,000 people at some of these matches and of a large grandstand being erected for the occasion.

More significantly, he took into his service some of the finest cricketers of his day so that they could enrich the game in Kent. Among them were the great batsman Joseph Miller; George Ring, who was Mann's whipper-in; and James Aylward, one of the very best batsmen in England, whom Sir Horace poached from Hambledon. It must be admitted that when Mann acquired Aylward in 1779, the great cricketer was 38 and perhaps past his prime.

Aylward was employed as Mann's bailiff, a post, according to Nyren and Beldham of Hambledon, for which he was ill suited. Their view is given substance by the fact that, within a few years, Aylward was the landlord of the White Horse in Bridge.

In the famous match at Bourne in 1773, Kent against Surrey, to which we have already alluded, the name of the Duke of Dorset appears at the head of the Kent list; he top-scored in the first innings with 25 out of 63. John Frederick Sackville was a year junior to Mann, but surviving scores would suggest that he was a better batsman. In August 1774, he hit 77 as Kent, with three 'given' men, beat Hampshire by an innings. This was a huge score in those days. The game was played at Sevenoaks, where he later gave The Vine by deed of trust to be a cricket ground forever.

Like Mann, he employed many noted cricketers on his estate. Joseph Miller, who hit 95 in the same match in which Dorset scored his 77, was one of his gamekeepers before moving into Mann's service. Dorset also employed William Yalden, the first of the great wicketkeepers, a man whose career was long, but who, according to Nyren, could not always be trusted for he would resort to trickery.

It is believed that Dorset's collection of professionals cost him in the region of £1,000 a year, but, as well as this expense, he wagered heavily on the game. He was, of course, a member of the Hambledon Club and also the White Conduit Club which gave birth to the MCC.

Although a friend of the main artistic figures of his age – he was a pallbearer at the funeral of Joshua Reynolds – Dorset was 'not distinguished for mental vigour or literary attainment', but he was briefly a Member of Parliament in Kent in 1768 before succeeding to the title on the death of his uncle the following year. Later the Duke was for six years ambassador extraordinary to the court of France, sensibly leaving that country at the start of its Revolution in 1789.

His real qualities, however, lay in other directions. He was described as having raven locks and wearing a milk white vest which allured 'a crowd of feminine spectators to the new pastime'. The excitement he engendered in the opposite sex was rumoured to have extended to Marie Antoinette although the memoirs of one of the Queen's ladies in waiting claimed that her majesty was so virtuous that she would not take a bath naked, so abhorrent was she of the sins of the flesh.

Surprisingly, he is credited with introducing from France that most English of habits, the taking of afternoon tea, so that he may well lay claim to instituting the tea interval into the game of cricket.

His patronage of the game had been immense, and there is no indication that his interest lessened during his years in France. In 1769 when John Minshull hit what many believe to be the first century in the history of the game, Dorset immediately engaged him as a gardener on his estate at Knole for a salary of eight shillings a week, and such engagements were to be of pleasure and value to the Duke. In 1789, he employed Yalden to bring a team to Paris for a cricket match. Yalden gathered together some of the best players of the day, and the side was led by the Earl of Tankerville.

Tankerville was to Surrey cricket what Dorset and Mann had been to Kent cricket. He employed the great bowler 'Lumpy' Stevens as a gardener, and another fine player, William Bedster, was a butler. Yalden had also been in his service before moving to Knole. He was himself a good batsman, and his home at Walton-on-Thames throbbed with the game. He was also a Privy Councillor and Joint Postmaster-General.

Tankerville and his side set out for France, but at Dover they were met by the Duke of Dorset who was fleeing from the French

Revolution. Dorset was taken to Bourne Park where he was entertained by Sir Horace Mann. The following day, they watched Kent play Surrey. These men had their priorities, and none have given stronger substance to G. M. Trevelyan's assertion, 'If the French noblesse had been capable of playing cricket with their peasants, their chateaux would never have been burned.'

Dorset's interest in cricket appears to have waned after 1791, but he was not in the best of mental health, and when he died in 1799, at the age of 54, his condition had been unstable for the best part of two years.

His friend Sir Horace Mann outlived him by 15 years, but his end was not the happiness that he might have expected or deserved. He finds a place in this chronicle because he was Member of Parliament for Maidstone from 1774 to 1784, and for Sandwich from 1790 to 1807, but 'his life was rather dedicated to pleasure than business', and he went bankrupt. His last years were devoted to whist, and he spent his time in Bath and Margate where he died in 1814.

His passion for the game was intense, and John Nyren, in *The Cricketers of My Time*, gives a delightful picture of Sir Horace's involvement. Nyren recalls the prowess of Noah Mann, the great left-hander who was adept with both bat and ball and who felt that he should have batted higher in the order than he was generally allowed to at Hambledon. He was a tremendous hitter and very quick between the wickets.

Nyren states that in a match between Hambledon and All England, the Hampshire men needed a considerable number of runs to win the match. 'It became quite apparent that the game would be closely fought. Mann kept on worrying old Nyren to let him go in, and although he became quite indignant at his constant refusal, our General knew what he was about in keeping him back. At length, when the last but one was out, he sent Mann in, and there were ten runs to get. The sensation now all over the ground was greater than anything of the kind I ever witnessed before or since. All knew the state of the game, and many thousands were hanging upon this narrow point.

There was Sir Horace Mann walking about outside the ground cutting down the daisies with his stick – a habit with him when he was agitated; the old farmers leaning forward upon their tall old staves, and the whole multitude perfectly still.'

Noah Mann hit Lumpy for six and eventually won the match, and Nyren does not record Sir Horace's reactions. On another occasion, Sir Horace offered his huntsman, John Ring, £10 a year for life if he could bat out the innings and make the runs required to win. Ring fell four short we are told, but it is not difficult to see why Sir Horace went bankrupt.

His political career left no great imprint upon the life of the country, but when, 28 years after his death, Canterbury Week came into being, there were those who tried to rekindle the joys he had given. *Bell's Life*, the publication most widely read by sportsmen of the day, regretted that 'the good, the merry olden days of Sir Horace Mann are now gone by'. There have been many greater politicians than Sir Horace, and many greater cricketers, but few have earned such generous epitaphs. He lived life to the full, and other men were richer for knowing him.

Other names who have a strong Kentish ring should now be recorded. William Deedes played for the county in 1822-23 as well as in Gentlemen v Players matches over similar years, as a swift underarm bowler and successful bat. In 1831 he was MCC president and later Secretary and Treasurer during the early years of the Band of Brothers, who have subsequently been a significant force in Kent County Cricket. This post no doubt arose from his rank at the East Kent Yeomanry from whom the BB's emerged in the 1850s.

William Deedes – often called the Elder – first entered Parliament for East Kent in 1845 and held the seat with an eight-month pause in 1857 until his death in 1862. Although a Conservative, the Deedes family papers note that he was never strictly speaking a 'party man'. This won him respect but failed – as so often – to result in office. Andre Maurois's *Disraeli* records the story of Lord Stanley declining to form a Government on the death of Peel in 1850 by saying there was insufficient talent in the party. One of the whips suggested there were several men of worth waiting to be called at the Carlton Club, including Deedes. "Pshaw!" came the reply, "These are not names I can put before the Queen."

The Deedes name was held in better esteem by the Men of Kent. One of William the Elder's 12 children, William the Younger, (1834-87) also represented East Kent from 1876 until his death. As a soldier he served through the Crimean War and the Indian Mutiny, later becoming Brigade Major at Aldershot. We know less of his cricketing skills except that he played for the Gentlemen of Kent in 1853 and graced many a Kent Cricket Week subsequently.

The Deedes name lives on in Parliament with the latest William, who served as Conservative MP for Ashford (1950-74) and now in the Upper House as Baron Deedes of Aldington. As a distinguished editor of the *Daily Telegraph* (1974-85), he supported its excellent cricket coverage but lists his recreation as 'golf'. Not so his son, another in the journalist line, who puts 'cricket' amongst others in that category but neither were able, in these changed times, to play in the first-class game.

William Ward was never a candidate for bankruptcy. Born in Islington in 1787, the son of a London merchant who owned a considerable amount of land on the Isle of Wight, Ward was educated at Winchester and, from an early age, was destined for the world of commerce.

Having spent the earlier part of his business career in a banking house in Antwerp, he returned to England, entered the stock exchange and went into partnership with his father. In 1817, at the age of 30, he became a director of the Bank of England, his knowledge of foreign commerce and exchange being his particular strength.

William Ward's success in business was mirrored by his prowess as a sportsman. From his days at Winchester, he had been renowned as an athlete, and he was an influential member of MCC. He supported Thomas Lord in his endeavours to establish a ground, and when the third, last and most famous of Lord's grounds came into being in 1814, Ward played in the inaugural 'great' match at the new venue in

St John's Wood. MCC beat Hertfordshire by an innings, and Ward scored 10.

Six years later, playing for MCC against Norfolk at Lord's, on 24 July, he hit 278. It was the first double century and the highest score made on the famous ground for 105 years. Ward's record finally fell to Percy Holmes who hit 315 not out for Yorkshire against Middlesex in June 1925.

Renowned as a hard-hitting batsman who always used a 4lbs bat, Ward established another record in 1825 when he made 102 for the Gentlemen against the Players, again at Lord's. This was the only occasion in the history of these famous matches that the game was spread over four days, and it was the first on which a century was scored for the Gentlemen. Ward was hit on the finger and forced to retire hurt, but the Gentlemen, who played 16 men including the 'given' professional Matthews, went on to win by 72 runs.

Two years later, Ward was left unbeaten on 96, with the next highest scorer in the Gentlemen's 17 being P. H. Dyke with 18, and it was to be 43 years, in 1868, before another century was scored for the Gentlemen. The batsman on that occasion was one W. G. Grace.

William Ward played in the fixture until 1838 when he was 51. He scored 18, second highest scorer, and 8 in a low-scoring match. Five years before this, John Nyren had dedicated his famous book, the first cricket classic, *The Young Cricketer's Tutor*, to Ward. Nyren was proud and honoured that Ward accepted the dedication, for he considered Ward 'a countryman of my own – having lived in Hampshire' and 'as a cricketer, I consider you the most worthy man of the present day to reflect upon my choice as a patron'.

Ward was a man of 'high public worth and integrity', and Nyren, although he had not seen Ward play as much as he would have wished, pronounced him one of the safest players he had seen. 'The superiority of your rising so much above the ordinary standard in stature (your height, if I recollect, being six feet one inch), your extraordinary length of limb, your power and activity; to all of which, I may add, your perfect judgement of all points in the game; have given you the superior advantages in play, and entitle you to the character I have given.'

Not only was Ward superior among the amateur cricketers of his day, he was above all a driving force in the furtherance and prosperity of the game. His best remembered act was to save Lord's.

In 1825, Thomas Lord, nearing 70, hinted that he was becoming dissatisfied with the small amount of profit he was receiving from his venture. He told the Marylebone Club that he had received permission from the Eyre Estate to develop seven pairs of houses on the ground. The space that would be left for cricket would not amount to more than 150 square yards. Ward's response to this dramatic news was immediate. He asked Lord how much he wanted to save the ground from the property developers, and he wrote Lord a cheque for the £5,000 he requested. Lord retired to the country, but his name was retained on the ground he had founded although Ward was now the owner.

There was an immediate tragedy, for, in 1825, the pavilion at Lord's burned down in rather mysterious circumstances. Ward had just had the building extended and redecorated, and the fire took not only the pavilion but the records and trophies of the Marylebone Club and a valuable wine-cellar. Undaunted, Ward had the pavilion rebuilt and ready for the 1826 season, the speed with which he had the job accomplished surprising many members.

His efforts on behalf of the game were not restricted to Lord's and the MCC, for Ward was an instigator in the foundation of the Surrey Club in 1845. He presided over the inaugural meeting at the Horns Tavern, in the absence of the Hon H. Ponsonby, and when it was decided unanimously that the Surrey County Club should be formed, he proposed the toast of success and prosperity to the club. He also implored the new committee to look for a good wicketkeeper, emphasising the importance of a first-rate man in the job. 'Such a man not only taught an excellent lesson for domestic life, but he taught a lesson in cricket: he taught a man to "keep at home", a practice which was equally valuable in their respective points – keeping at home was a valuable ingredient to true domestic felicity, and it constantly, in cricket, made a man play properly.'

Ward was a man of strong family values. His son entered the church and was instrumental in establishing cricket at Fenner's. His four daughters were to be concerned with him in the business negotiations which resulted in his releasing his hold on Lord's.

This was in 1835, but by that time, much had happened in Ward's life. As we have said, he became a director of the Bank of England in 1817, and, as a powerful and much respected figure in the City of London, he was asked to stand as Tory candidate for that constituency in the election of June 1826. He was duly elected, and, in 1830, at the request of the Prime Minister, the Duke of Wellington, he became chairman of the committee appointed to investigate the affairs of the East India Company, preparatory to opening of trade with China.

The same year, Earl Grey succeeded Wellington as Prime Minister, and, discontented at the spirit of reform that was abroad in the land, William Ward declined to stand for Parliament. In 1835, he was persuaded to change his mind and was again the Tory candidate for the City of London, but moods had changed. Peel's first ministry was to last only a year, and Melbourne and the Whigs swept to power for a second time. Ward was defeated by his Whig opponent. Hurt, he announced that he was retiring from public life.

His life in cricket continued although it was in that year, 1835, that he sold the lease of Lord's to J. H. Dark. Ward received £2,000, and he and his daughters were to receive £425 a year for the duration of the unexpired lease, 59 years. It has been suggested that it was a reverse in his fortunes that caused Ward to sell Lord's, but we should remember the sale coincided with his disillusioned political retirement.

From cricket, he did not retire. He played until 1845, four years before his death at the age of 62. A first-class career of 4,000 runs in 130 matches shows he was no mean performer. He also took 49 wickets with his lobs.

Men like Ward, Horace Mann and Richmond, and others who were the social, commercial or financial leaders in their communities, invariably came to represent those communities in Parliament. It was general, too, as part of their standing that they should be good

Pioneers

horsemen and competent cricketers. Did not Lord Chesterfield, in
1774, in one of those letters of instruction to his son, plead that if the
boy had the right ambition, he would desire to excel all other boys of
his age at cricket?

It is not difficult to understand why the game seized the imagination
of the public. It was the province of peer and commoner alike, a mutual
meeting ground. As G. M. Trevelyan noted, cricket had enlarged both
its geographic and social boundaries by the beginning of the 18th
century. By the middle of that century, 'noblemen, gentlemen and
clergy' were making 'butchers, cobblers or tinkers their companions' at
cricket.

'Village cricket spread fast through the land. In those days, before it
became scientific, cricket was the best game in the world to watch, with
its rapid sequence of amusing incidents, each ball a potential crisis!
Squire, farmer, blacksmith and labourer, with their women and
children came to see the fun, were at ease together and happy all the
summer afternoon.'

Politicians, too, were part of this idyllic picture that Trevelyan
paints, and as the 19th century progressed, their numbers on the
cricketing scene grew appreciably.

Founders and
Saviours

LET us first consider the Grimstons. Historians challenge the claim that Sylvester de Grimston was the standard bearer to William the Conqueror, but none can dispute that the Grimstons were active in politics from the 17th century onwards.

Sir Harbottle Grimston, puritan and judge, was Speaker of the House of Commons in 1660. It was he who purchased the Gorhambury estate, near St Alban's, once the home of the Bacon family. Harbottle Grimston's grandson left the estate to his nephew William, who took the name of Grimston in lieu of his patronym Luckyn.

The Grimston family represented the Whig interest as members for St Alban's at various times between 1710 and 1761. They were not all noted for their sagacity and political acumen. William, appointed Viscount Grimston in 1719, was attacked both by the cartoonists, as an ass wearing a coronet, and by no less a person than the great poet Alexander Pope.

In his youth, William Grimston had written a rather foolish play, *The Lawyer's Fortune*, and, in his *Second Satire of the Second Book of Horace*, Pope refers to him in the couplet:

'Shades, that to BACON could retreat afford,
Become the portion of a booby Lord.'

It was his grandson James who broke with the Whig tradition, being Tory MP for St Alban's from 1783 until 1784 when he became the representative for Herts until 1790 when he was created Baron Verulam of Gorhambury.

The Tory connection was now a strong one. James Walter Grimston, educated at Harrow and at Christ Church College, Oxford, was MP for St Alban's, 1802 to 1808, and in 1815 was created First Earl of Verulam. He was Cupbearer at the coronation of George IV in July 1821, but, his chief interest to us is that he fathered four sons who appeared in important cricket matches of the day and were noted players.

Three of the boys followed their father to Harrow and Oxford. The eldest, James Walter, who succeeded to the title in 1845, was up at Oxford between 1828 and 1830, but there was a match against Cambridge only in the second of those years, and he did not play in it. In addition to matches for the Gentlemen (1836-39) and MCC (1830-43), he appeared for the Hertfordshire XIs of his time, and shared with his brothers the desire to establish a county club in Hertfordshire.

He was the Tory member for St Alban's, 1830-31, for Newport, Cornwall, 1831-32, and for Hertfordshire from 1832 until the time he succeeded to the title. As the Second Earl of Verulam, he continued to play cricket at a high level, and his final important match appears to have been for Married against Single in 1849. A first-class career batting average of 10.60 from 21 matches stands on the record.

Edward Harbottle Grimston was three years junior to his elder brother, and he first appeared at Lord's in 1827, playing for Harrow against Eton at the age of 15. He got his blue at Oxford in 1836, the only year during his period of residence when the match against Cambridge was played. E. H. Grimston top-scored in the Oxford first innings with 33 out of 100. The standard of the wicket can be judged from the fact that of the 479 runs scored in the match, 95 were byes. Oxford won by 121 runs.

E.H. was Tory MP for St Alban's, 1835-41, but he entered the church in 1841 when he became Rector of Pebmarsh in Essex to which, in 1845, was added the living at Great Henny.

He was described as 'one who loved cricket and was himself universally beloved'. Haygarth considered that he had one of the best styles ever seen. He was not a hard hitter, but he was upright, forward, and scientifically correct. A powerful and fit man, he stood 6ft and weighed 12st. As late as 1849, he made 69 not out and 50 for MCC against the Auberies, on the Essex-Suffolk border, and he was batting against such formidable bowlers as Lillywhite, Diver and Royston.

He was also a useful under-arm medium-pace bowler. His cricket, for MCC, Hertfordshire and the Essex XIs of the time, spanned some 30 seasons although he gave up playing in the important matches at Lord's and elsewhere once he entered the church. Thirty first-class matches with an average of 13.65 was his record before religion took over.

Edward's son, Walter Edward, was also a notable cricketer, a hard-hitting batsman and wicketkeeper who played for Hertfordshire, Essex, Suffolk and I Zingari sides. He was also Master of the Essex Hounds.

The youngest of the First Earl of Verulam's cricketing sons, Francis Sylvester, broke with family tradition in that he went from Harrow to Cambridge where he won his blue in all three years, 1843 to 1845, as a capable wicketkeeper and batsman. He played for MCC, and, like his brothers, for sides which were labelled Hertfordshire or Essex. A large man – he was 6ft 3ins and weighed 15½st – F. S. Grimston also entered the church and became Rector of Wakes Colne in Essex where he died at the age of 43. He seldom played at Lord's or in important matches after his time at Cambridge, and it seems that he was less inclined to political activity than his brothers. He was certainly less active than Robert, born in 1816, and six years his senior.

The Hon Robert Grimston was never a Member of Parliament, and his biographer, Frederick Gale, suggests that it was a mercy he was not, 'as he most certainly would have called things by their right names, in a very intelligible manner, and if anyone had deviated from strict truth or shuffled, he would have been "down" upon him pretty quick.' But even though he was never elected to serve, this forthright eccentric, who believed sparring to be an integral part of education and who would box a few rounds with his dinner guests before he fed them, demands a place in this chronicle.

He was averse to change of all kinds, severely condemned betting and gambling and was a determined old-fashioned Tory. An utterly fearless rider to hounds and a successful gentleman jockey, Robert Grimston had a political conviction that surpassed his passion for horses. Gale tells how he refused to buy one horse that he fancied because it had been sired by a stallion called Free Trader, and rejected another fine horse when he learned its name was Gladstone. His love of horses and the chase was second only to his devotion to the game of cricket.

He entered the chambers of Alexander Sidebottom when he left Oxford in 1838 and was called to the Bar in 1843. One of his close companions in chambers was Frederick Ponsonby, later Lord Bessborough, another passionate Old Harrovian and, although a cricketer of limited accomplishment, a devotee of the game and one of the founders of I Zingari. Both Grimston and Ponsonby were in the Gentlemen's side that beat the Players in 1842. Grimston appeared twice more in the fixture, the last occasion being in 1849.

There seems to have been an element of eccentricity in his cricket as in other areas of his life. Haygarth described him as '...a remarkably steady batsman combined with occasional hard forward hitting, and generally successful against fast bowling, especially against that of the late A. Mynn, off whom he made several fine innings. When opposed to Mr A. Mynn he always took two bats to the wicket, one to play that gentleman's bowling, which was of a larger size, and another of the usual dimensions to hit all the rest.'

Certainly, Robert Grimston had his successes against Mynn, and he told the good-natured Alfred that he had named his heavy bat 'Mynn's Master'. He was in the Gentlemen's side which beat the Players by an innings in 1849, and was one of the first members of I Zingari. He was, in fact, honorary treasurer, but as the subscription to the famous club was nil, his office was not an arduous one.

He played for I Zingari many times on their country tours, but it is as an enthusiast and supporter of the game rather than as a player that he is best remembered. He was the father of cricket at Harrow, giving much of his time to coaching the boys and offering hospitality and matches at Gorhambury. Indeed, his passion was such that he seemed to carry a vendetta against the cricketers of Eton and was eventually 'warned off' for his over zealous management of affairs from the boundary.

Another of Robert Grimston's beliefs was that the smoother grounds, the pads, gloves and boundaries of his later years were responsible for the breeding of cowards. "A man had to rely entirely on his nerve and quickness of hand and eye, and if he had not all these, he was fit for nothing."

Grimston's old Toryism in cricket was further evidenced by Robert Thoms, one of the finest umpires and a great patron of Middlesex, who was asked by James Dark, the ruling spirit of Lord's, for use of his mowing machine, 'a large and good one', which was used to keep down the grass on the pitch at Primrose Hill. The machine was taken to Lord's, and it was used to mow the wickets before ten in the morning.

To the surprise of Thoms and Dark, Grimston arrived on the ground. He seemed to assess the situation at once, ignored his two friends and strode to the top of the ground, close to where the printing office now stands and where some navvies were working. He asked them if they wanted to earn a sovereign, and when they replied eagerly that they did, he told them to get their pickaxes and 'smash that infernal machine up'.

Jordan, the groundsman, stood between the navvies and the machine and prevented the destruction. Thoms and his two workmen took the mower back to Primrose Hill while Grimston and Dark whispered to each other 'in the most frantic manner'. Thoms later remarked to Dark that, being a huntsman, Grimston must have scented the machine from where he lived, for what else could have brought him to Lord's so early that morning. "That was the first time a mowing machine was used at Lord's, and not again for years after; for the Hon Robert Grimston, like many others, believed in sheep grazing."

He was not at ease as a barrister, scorning those social contacts which would have brought lucrative business, and he virtually gave up the law after his passionate involvement in the election for the Hertfordshire seats in 1852. He eschewed all engagements, business and pleasure, including cricket at Harrow, during the contest, but the Liberals triumphed. Bulwer Lytton, later Lord Lytton, the novelist and playwright, was the foremost of their candidates.

Robert Grimston's death was as interesting as his life. He suffered a series of strokes which ended his hunting and virtually ended his coaching days. He lived with his brother the Earl, at Gorhambury, and one evening said that he would not be down for dinner, but would eat in his room. In the middle of dinner, his butler broke the news diplomatically to the Earl: "Mr Robert is not alive."

What would he think today with motor mowers at Lord's and helmets everywhere? His greatest grief would, however, be that the more recent generations of Grimstons have been educated at Eton.

His friend, first colleague in the study of law and co-coach and mentor of Harrow cricket, Lord Bessborough outlived him by 11 years. With his brother, Spencer Cecil Brabazon Ponsonby, later Ponsonby-Fane, and J. L. Baldwin, he had founded I. Zingari of which Grimston was the honorary treasurer. Ponsonby-Fane was closely connected with politics, holding many important posts, including those of Private Secretary to Lord Palmerston, to the Earl of Clarendon and to Earl Granville. He was also Comptroller of the Lord Chamberlain's Office. This was the age when those who held high office played cricket. This was the time when Lords and Commons Cricket came into being.

As Eric Bullus MP, who played regularly in their teams from 1950-74, asserts, Lords and Commons Cricket is older than the County Championship and older than the majority of county clubs. There are few early records of Lords and Commons Cricket, but substantial evidence of the match against I Zingari, at Vincent Square, 22 June 1850. Ponsonby-Fane played for I Zingari, and Lords and Commons Cricket included the Earl of Verulam. In his younger days, Verulam – Harrow and Oxford – had played for Gentlemen against Players.

Lilleywhite described him as 'formerly one of the first hitters ever seen, who continued his hitting with a good defence'. An I Zingari account of his appearance at what was to become the spiritual home of Lords and Commons Cricket, through the courtesy of its Westminster School owners, ran as follows: 'The reappearance of Lord Verulam in flannels and bat in hand, gave great satisfaction to those whose memory carried them to the top of the tennis court at Lord's, o'er which in days gone by he drove a cricket ball; his power of leg-hitting appeared to have retained a corner in his memory.' In fact, he scored 4 and 0 as the Houses of Lords and Commons (with Wisden) made 75 and 132, and I Zingari totalled 97 in a match that was unfinished.

Lords and Commons Cricket were to become noted in the years ahead as not averse to including the odd ringer. They certainly seem to have started early in being allowed to play John Wisden as a given man and there have been few better subsequently. In 1850, he was the most formidable bowler in the land, and three weeks after the match at Vincent Square, he took all ten wickets, clean bowled, when he represented the North against the South. For Lords and Commons Cricket, he contented himself with nine I Zingari scalps, seven bowled, two caught and bowled. The tenth wicket, T. E. L. Mostyn, later Lord Mostyn, was run out.

Also appearing for Lords and Commons was one Lord Charles Russell, a Whig MP for Bedfordshire 1832-41, whose scores of 0 and 1 indicate a modest cricketing potential. He was better known as the half-brother of Prime Minister Lord John Russell, but also a player for and president of the MCC as well as acting as Serjeant-at-Arms for the Commons over a number of years. Lord Russell's judgement of the game was, however, not to be doubted. Speaking in 1879 to mark W. G. Grace's testimonial he said: "If you want to see Mr Grace play cricket, I would ask you to look at him playing one ball. You all know the miserable tame effect of the ball hitting the bat instead of the bat hitting the ball, whether acting on the offensive or the defensive. In playing a ball, Mr Grace puts every muscle into it from the sole of his foot to the crown of his head." It is a picture of the Champion in action strikingly similar to C. B. Fry's famous description many years later.

These early Lords and Commons fixtures provide invaluable intelligence on parliamentary cricket of the day but the material is sadly limited. Games at Lord's and The Oval are covered in following years but there are clearly many gaps in the record. An I Zingari v Lords and Commons match at Lord's in 1857 is interesting, however, because the 19-year-old Earl of Coventry makes his appearance. Noted as a 'Lord, slashing hitter and slow lob bowler' – an interesting mixture of characteristics – he had played for Worcestershire. Records of his achievements then are vague but two relatives later appeared for Worcestershire – the Hon Henry Thomas and later the Hon John Bonynge, who played in 75 matches and captained them in 1929-30.

Another relation is more famous – H.T.'s brother the Hon Charles John Coventry. He appeared briefly for Worcestershire but also for England. These were the first Test Matches against South Africa, played at Port Elizabeth and Cape Town in 1889 and they comprise his entire first-class career. At least both were resounding victories and he had the distinction of playing under C. A. (later Sir Aubrey) Smith. It must have been some compensation for twice batting at number 10 and scoring only 13 runs. No doubt the Earl of Coventry would have been pleased with his relatives' records. He died in 1930, having been a peer for 86 years.

Reverting to the 1850 Vincent Square match, the highest score was made by H. M. Curteis who carried out his bat for 34 in the parliamentarians' second innings. Herbert Mascall Curteis was Master of the East Sussex Fox Hounds and MP for Rye (1847-52), as was his father before him. He was a genial man who played 43 times for Sussex over a period of 14 years, 1846 to 1860. He was a cricketer of moderate accomplishment, but one of the saviours of Sussex County Cricket Club.

Curteis, whose two sons appeared for Sussex, played for Oxford in the Varsity matches of 1841 and 1842. He 'bagged a pair' in the first match and made five in each innings of the second. Cambridge won the game by eight runs. Their top scorer was J. R. R. Bulwer who was to become Conservative MP for Ipswich (1874-80) and Cambridgeshire (1881-85) and to decline the post of Chief Justice for Madras. The highest score in the match was 40 not out by R. Garth of Oxford in the second innings. He became Tory MP for Guildford (1866-68), appeared in a game for a Surrey XI and was later Chief Justice of Bengal.

These early Varsity matches were a breeding ground for politicians and churchmen, but they were not given first-class status in the main records. More than half the players in the inaugural game in 1827 took holy orders while E. Horsman of Cambridge became a Member of Parliament and fought a duel with a fellow MP whom he accused of secretly having Chartist sympathies and speaking disrespectfully of the Queen. Both men emerged from the quarrel unscathed.

Unlike G. P. Ottey of Rugby who played three times for Cambridge with distinction between 1847 and 1849 and then was lost to cricket as he became Member of Parliament first for Chippenham and then for North Wiltshire, Curteis did appear in major cricket for Sussex although rarely in the stronger fixtures. Invariably he batted at number nine, ten or 11, but he was a most liberal supporter of Sussex cricket. His influence on the government and committee of the club was of far greater value and significance than his performances on the field where his career average was 6.82, highest score 29.

By the middle of the 19th century, cricket in Sussex, as elsewhere, was at a low ebb. The Sussex club had 'dwindled into insignificance'. Under Bridger Stent, a man of passionate commitment to the county, who became secretary and the president, the Second Earl of Sheffield, Sussex County Cricket Club was reorganised and revived. In 1869, Herbert Curteis took over as president and remained in that position for ten years which were, by no means, the easiest in the club's history.

Within months of Curteis becoming president, Stent died, and the following year, the old Brunswick Ground on which Sussex had played their matches was lost. In a phrase ominously familiar over the years, it had become an eligible plot.

Curteis was one of those whose industry and enthusiasm found Sussex a new ground, part of the old Stanhope Estate directly north of the Brunswick ground. Curteis was one of the lessees of this ground at Hove to which Sussex moved all their goods and chattels, including every turf from the Royal Brunswick pitch. It was ready for play at the beginning of the 1872 season.

When Curteis stood down seven years later he was succeeded as president by Henry North Holroyd Pevensey, Third Earl of Sheffield.

Sheffield's claims for inclusion in this chronicle on the political side are clear. He was born in London, educated at Eton and joined the Diplomatic Service. He was sent to the Embassy in Constantinople in 1851, and later became Attache at the Embassy in Copenhagen. He returned to Constantinople in 1853 and was there until 1856, being in residence there during the worst period of the Crimean War. He returned to England and became MP for East Sussex from 1857 to 1865. In 1876, he became Third Earl of Sheffield on the death of his father and inherited the estate at Sheffield Park where he had developed and continued to develop a most beautiful cricket ground.

His credentials on the cricketing side, at least as a player, are less impressive. In Lewes, in September 1854, he was one of Sixteen of Sussex who lost to the United England XI by eight wickets. Batting at number 13, Viscount Pevensey was bowled Dean 0, caught Adams, bowled Dean 0 – hardly a major first-class achievement. This was the only match of substance in which he appeared but if there were limitations in his playing ability, as a benefactor he had no equal. He held sway over Sussex cricket for a quarter of a century, being president until 1897 and returning for another year in 1904. For all his generosity and endeavour, he was often subject to criticism, and he tendered his resignation at the beginning of the 1887 season after receiving several abusive letters. The men of Sussex rallied to his defence and signed a petition imploring him to continue as president. His worth to the county was immeasurable.

He employed Alfred Shaw, the veteran Nottinghamshire bowler, as coach, and he had coaching wickets prepared at Sheffield Park, Hove,

Eastbourne and Hastings. He paid Shaw and the expenses of the young men who were selected for coaching.

Alfred Shaw acted as something of a private secretary to Lord Sheffield and accompanied him on many of his trips abroad. With cricket ever in his mind, Sheffield had the idea when in a fjord near Spitzbergen of playing a match on the deck of the ship, the *Lusitania*, under the midnight sun in a northern summer. According to Shaw: 'Wickets were pitched, a ball improvised, and at a quarter to 12 on the night of August 12, 1894, this strange game commenced. Of course, I had to bowl, and Lord Sheffield opened the batting. Between a quarter to 12 and half-past 12, I had bowled out practically all the gentlemen passengers and officers, fully 40 all told.'

His Lordship collected cricket curios on his travels, and these were part of the glory of Sheffield Park where he often entertained the visiting Australian sides and allowed the public free admission. His generosity to his tenants and poor neighbours became legendary. He provided the nearby port of Newhaven with a cricket ground for the local club and a site for a town hall. He paid for special trains for children to be brought to visit Sheffield Park, and, having no children of his own, adopted several orphans of soldiers killed in the Boer War.

To Sussex cricket, as to those children, he was a life-line. A. D. Taylor, an historian of the Marylebone Club, wrote of him, and of Sussex: 'At one time the Club was in such difficulties that it would have been dissolved but for Lord Sheffield's timely help. He said: "Spend what money you like, and send the bill to me; I'll pay it." '

Nor was Lord Sheffield's generosity limited to Sussex cricket. In 1887-88, two 'England' sides toured Australia; one, known as Vernon's team, and captained by Hon M. B. Hawke, later Lord Hawke, was sponsored by the Melbourne Club; the other was a professional side under Lillywhite, Shaw and Shrewsbury, and was managed in conjunction with the New South Wales Association. The result of the twin tours was, inevitably, a financial disaster. Two Australian sides came to England within the next two years of those tours. Neither was overly impressive, with the result that cricket in Australia fell in popularity. The political in-fighting between Melbourne and Sydney did nothing to improve the standing of the game, and, by 1891, the general feeling was that only a tour by an England party of strength would revive interest.

No one in Australia was willing to finance the venture, but Lord Sheffield took on the task. He made the stipulation that he would not give his support unless W. G. Grace went as captain. Grace agreed, and, in fact, only Shrewsbury and Gunn, the Nottinghamshire batsmen, declined the terms that were offered. Two of the three Test matches that were played were won by Australia and attendances were good. The tour lost money – it cost Lord Sheffield £2,000 – but it did its job. Cricket was back in favour in Australia.

Lord Sheffield was rapturously received, and his name was to be permanently stamped on Australian cricket. On his arrival, he had offered a trophy to the value of £150 or thereabouts for competition by the three colonies in any way agreed upon by them. After deliberation, debate and considerable argument, the Sheffield Shield was first contested in 1892-93 and won by Victoria.

The title Earl of Sheffield had been given to the Third Earl's grandfather, John Holroyd, in recognition of his valiant defence of the Bank of England during a civil insurrection in 1780. One would doubt whether such an act would be so rewarded today, and certainly we do not know how fully the Third Earl interested himself in banking or even politics. He was a member of both Houses during his life-time, but it was his commitment to the game of cricket that was inexhaustible and most clearly definable. He was 72 years old when he was last president of Sussex, and he gave a gift of £100 to the county club when he finally stood down.

Lord Sheffield dedicated his life to cricket. There were others who, as we shall see, were able to combine the qualities of cricket and government.

Cricketers in
Government

THE men who were returned to Parliament in 1865 were of very much the same character as those elected in 1830. In 1833, there were 217 Members of Parliament who were the sons of peers or baronets; in 1860, there were 180. As late as 1880, there were 170, yet by then the complexion of Parliament had begun to change. It had become easier for men not of aristocratic parentage to reach very high political office.

Robert Peel had been the first son of a manufacturer to become Prime Minister, and Lord Melbourne had belonged to none of the aristocratic families, but it was not until after 1867 that more middle-class men came to predominate in cabinet office. While cabinet posts of importance were held by peers it meant that most members of the government had not been elected by any constituency. It meant also that debates in the House of Lords were of equal, if not greater, significance than those in the House of Commons. Governments were led mostly by men of the old aristocracy – Derby, Russell, Palmerston – who had their spokesmen in the House of Commons.

On three occasions, Benjamin Disraeli had served as the power in the Commons with the Earl of Derby as Prime Minister in the House of Lords. These three ministries were brief, as was Disraeli's first ministry, and, in 1868, Gladstone became Prime Minister.

Gladstone belonged to a Scottish merchant family from Liverpool; Disraeli, who became Prime Minister in 1874, was the son of a Jewish literary man and the grandson of a Jewish stockbroker. He was a man of fashion, charm and sensitivity who was a novelist of repute. Less well recorded is that he was the first Prime Minister to appoint three men with experience in first-class cricket as part of his government.

The first of these appointments was of Sir William Hart Dyke as Parliamentary Secretary to the Treasury. The Seventh Baronet was born at St Mary Cray, Kent, in 1837, and died in Dartford 94 years later. He had been a member of MCC for 74 years, and he was president of the club in 1880, as of Kent four years later. He was a noted rackets player, and one of the MCC tennis committee who drew up the laws for lawn tennis when the game was introduced to Lord's in 1875. Sir William had a lengthy Parliamentary career, sitting for West Kent 1865-68, for the mid Division of Kent 1868-85, and finally for the Dartford division 1885-1906. He was Conservative Chief Whip 1874-80.

Whatever Hart Dyke's claims as a rackets player and Parliamentarian, his standing as a first-class cricketer is rather tenuous. He appeared in only one match of importance, at the St Lawrence Ground in Canterbury in August 1863. He scored 9 and 33 for the Gentlemen of Kent against MCC who won by two wickets. The match was 12-a-side, and Hart Dyke batted number 12 in the first innings and number 11 in the second when he and M. A. Troughton added 87 for the tenth wicket. It was a considerable achievement as the Kent side had been bowled out for that score in their first innings. Dyke held two catches, but his name appeared no more in the great matches of his day. *Wisden* was to say of him at his death that he had gained 'little distinction at cricket', but he did remain in government office until the Conservatives fell in April 1880. Nor was that the end of his political career. He was Chief Secretary to Ireland in the Marquis of Salisbury's first ministry, which lasted from June 1885, to January 1886, and he was president of the Board of Education in Salisbury's second administration, which lasted from July 1886 until August 1892. Lord Hamilton's terms of office were to last even longer.

Lord George Francis Hamilton's claim to be recognised as a first-class cricketer is only marginally superior to Hart Dyke's. He was a hard-hitting right-handed batsman, and 'an active field, generally at cover-slip'. He was also 'an exceedingly straight and fast under-hand bowler'. In spite of the description that Haygarth gives of him, Hamilton failed to get into the Harrow side in 1862. Like Hart Dyke, he was a long-time member of MCC – 64 years – and succeeded Hart Dyke as president in 1881.

At this time, he was Conservative MP for the County of Middlesex, having been elected in 1868 when he was 23 years old, and he held the constituency until 1885 when, in the reconstruction, he became Member for the Ealing Division, a seat he held for the next 21 years.

His links with Middlesex were strong, although he was born in Brighton, for he had served on the committee of the old Prince's Club which had been home to Middlesex until it was developed for property. He was vice-president of the county club from 1876 until 1906 and also president of Kent in 1919.

He was to hold various government offices in a period that spanned 29 years. For the first four years of Disraeli's ministry, he was Under Secretary to the India Office, and from 1878 to 1880, president of the Board of Education. When the Conservatives were returned to office for seven months in 1885, Salisbury appointed him First Lord of the Admiralty, a post he retained during Salisbury's second ministry, 1886-92. His final appointment was as Secretary of State for India, 1895 until 1903.

If Lord Hamilton's status as a first-class cricketer has more substance than that of his government colleague Hart Dyke, it is because it is now generally accepted that we date first-class cricket from 1864, and it was in that year that Hamilton played in his one match of note. At Lord's, in June, he was in the MCC side that lost to Cambridge University by an innings. He batted at number seven, hit 2 and 5, and took 0-12 in his five overs. *Wisden* does credit him with a hat-trick for Peripatetics against West Kent, at Chislehurst, the same season, but that was not a match of first-class standing.

The interesting point regarding the one first-class match in which Lord Hamilton appeared is that three other politicians played in the same game – Lord Garlies, Thomas de Grey and H. M. Hyndman.

Lord Alan Plantagenet Stewart Garlies was to succeed as tenth Earl Galloway in 1873 by which time his appearances in first-class cricket were at an end. A Scot who was by chance born in London, he was president of MCC in 1858, the year in which he is first recorded as having played for the club in an important fixture. Five years earlier, he had first appeared in the Harrow side, and, in the match against Winchester, he had top-scored with innings of 17 and 23. He was known as being an energetic deep field and a steady bat with a hard forward drive who occasionally kept wicket. His steadiness was certainly in evidence in his second innings against Winchester, for his 23 occupied three hours 40 minutes, exceptionally slow at that time.

He top-scored with 18 in the second MCC innings of the match he played alongside Lord Hamilton, which was, in fact, his penultimate first-class appearance. He did play for Rutland, but he was Conservative Member of Parliament for Wigtownshire from 1868 until 1873 when he succeeded to the title. His five first-class matches yielded 96 runs at a 13.71 average.

Opposed to Hamilton and Garlies in the Cambridge University side of 1864 was Hon Thomas de Grey, later Sixth Baron Walsingham. As one of the steadiest bats in the Eton side of 1860 and 1861, he had never played in a losing team in any of the big matches. He was described as one of the finest fieldsmen of his day, especially at cover point, and he was reputed to be a batsman of supreme confidence with a very strong defence. It was said that he had two or three bowlers going at the same time in practice and would place a fourth stump on the off side to encourage them.

He won his blue as a freshman at Cambridge in 1862, and he appeared again in the Varsity match in 1863. He was in fine form the following season and but for rheumatism would have opened the innings against Oxford. He played in the trial matches in 1865, his fourth year at university, but his interest in the game seems to have declined, perhaps because in the same year he was elected Member of Parliament for West Norfolk. He held the seat until he became the Sixth Baron Walsingham in 1870. His last first-class match was for MCC against Oxford University in 1866, leaving him with an average of 14.62 from 15 matches.

He had been chosen for the Gentlemen against the Players while in his second year at Cambridge so that it was apparent that he was a cricketer held in high esteem, but he was a man of many talents and interests. He had what was reputed to be the finest collection in the world of smaller butterflies and moths, and this he presented to the Natural History Museum at South Kensington in 1910. A somewhat contrasting love of nature is his acknowledgement as the best game shot in Great Britain. It is doubtful if a record bag of 1,070 grouse in one day in August 1888, has ever been equalled. His serious cricket really ended with his university days.

The fourth – and in many ways the most interesting – politician to play in the match between MCC and Cambridge University in June 1864 was Henry Mayers Hyndman. He was a wealthy man. His grandfather had made a fortune in the West Indies, and his father had added to it. Although he gave much of the fortune to the Anglican Church, he left enough for Henry to live on comfortably for the rest of his life.

Hyndman was privately educated and then went up to Trinity College, Cambridge, in 1861. He was more interested in cricket than study, and although he absorbed some liberal thought at Trinity, it was not enough to dent his conservative upbringing and long-standing family ties to the Tory party.

There was, however, a bitter disappointment for him at Cambridge in that, although he played first-class cricket for the university, he did not get his blue. There were those who put sinister interpretations on Hyndman's response to his disappointment. Barbara Tuchman, the

American historian, in her study of the world in the years leading up to the First World War, *The Proud Tower*, unkindly suggests that there was 'some justification for the friends who said that Hyndman, a cricketer, had adopted Socialism out of spite against the world because he was not included in the Cambridge XI'.

Certainly, Hyndman had every reason to feel hurt by his non-inclusion for the Oxford game. In that 1864 season, he played three times for Sussex and finished on the winning side each time. He hit 58 against Hampshire when he and James Lillywhite jnr added 106 for the third wicket, and followed this with 6 and 62 against Middlesex. His second innings 62 certainly made possible Sussex's victory by three wickets.

Sussex, and Hyndman, were less successful the following season, but by now Hyndman was studying for the Bar. He found the work too demanding and decided to concentrate on cricket. He played eight matches in 1865, the last against Kent at Hastings in the September. That was the end of his first-class career – 13 matches at an average of 16.26.

Fate now took control of him. In 1866, he left England for Italy and was unexpectedly caught up in the Italian war with Austria over Venice. He became war correspondent for the *Pall Mall Gazette* when he experienced the horrors of the battle for the first time. He was deeply affected and became ill after a visit to a front-line hospital. He abhorred violence, but he approved of Italian nationalist aspirations and this led him to study European nationalism. He visited Garibaldi, Mazzini and the Hungarian revolutionary Louis Kossuth, and he had the greatest praise for the statecraft of Cavour.

His attraction to revolution, but his dislike of war and respect for traditional policies shaped his ideas on the role of socialism. He returned to Great Britain and argued a closer union between Britain and self-governing colonies. He went to Australia to test his theories on the problems of empire.

Having visited the United States, whose variety of universal suffrage he saw as dangerous, he returned to London in 1871 and championed the beneficial results of British imperialism while demanding a greater autonomy to the colonies and an intelligent reorganisation of the empire.

He wrote on foreign affairs for the *Pall Mall Gazette* and stood as an Independent for Marylebone in 1880. He sought support from the local Radical Association, but Gladstone denounced him as a 'closet Tory' and, facing certain defeat, he withdrew his candidature. Undaunted, he concentrated on building a political career. He was impressed by what he read of the German socialist Ferdinand Lasalle and of the political skill which had brought about social reforms from Bismark for the benefit of the German working class.

Lasalle had learned from Marx, and Hyndman sought to repeat the process in England. He met Marx, but he could not accept his view on revolution or on the Chartist movement. He visited Disraeli and put forward his ideas for the reorganisation of the British Empire. Disraeli warned him that his ideas were unacceptable to the Conservative Party.

Hyndman, hostile to the Liberals, then turned to the working class Radical Clubs as the only source of support for his ideas, but they showed suspicion at his wealthy background. He persevered, opposed the Liberal Party's Irish Coercion Bill, supported the striking Yorkshire miners and gradually won some support, particularly from the Radical MP Joseph Cowen who saw a chance to oppose Joseph Chamberlain.

In March 1881, Hyndman's Democratic Federation formally came into being. Being middle-class in structure and financed by Hyndman himself, it aroused the suspicions of the London workers. In truth, England's first socialist party was launched without either mass support or any truly socialist programme except for the demand for the nationalisation of the land. But after the loss of moderate radicals and the strengthening of ideals, belief began to grow, the most notable acquisition being the enrolment of William Morris.

By 1884, with the publication of pamphlets and the discussion at conferences, conversion to socialism was complete. Now came the internal strife of the Social Democratic Federation over personalities and policies. Hyndman was an able writer and speaker, but he was seen as vain and authoritarian. There was a split between the right, led by Hyndman and his call for parliamentary action, and the left, led most unwillingly by Morris and the call for social agitation.

Hyndman's patriotic support of Gordon in the Sudan and his refusal to speak at a meeting at Marx's grave brought matters to a head. The executive voted 10 to 8 that they had no confidence in Hyndman. The outcome was that the ten resigned and left a weakened organisation. Unbowed, the Federation entered three candidates in the General Election of 1885, but they were prejudiced by a smear of 'Tory Gold' and polled only 657 votes between them. In the party reorganisation that followed, with depression, unemployment and riots as a backdrop, there was a shift to the left.

Hyndman always believed that revolution would happen 'at ten o'clock next Monday morning', and he once told Shaw that he could not have continued had he not held this belief. His upbringing had bred him to arrogance, but his socialist convictions were sincere, and he devoted the major part of his life and fortune to his beliefs, albeit he was often the victim of his own paradoxes.

He died in 1921, left somewhat shattered by the First World War and by the revolution in Russia. Perhaps he was broken, too, by the fact that England had just lost eight Test matches in succession in Australia and that English cricket was at its lowest ebb. Would his life have been different had he been awarded his blue at Cambridge? It is a doubtful but interesting thought. Despite never sitting in Parliament, Hyndman is certainly worth a place in these pages.

We have digressed disgracefully from Disraeli's second ministry, 1874, and from his third cricketing appointment to a government office, the Rt Hon Edward Stanhope who played once for Kent in 1861 and appeared in the last of his three matches of importance for MCC some 18 years later. In 1859, he had been a member of an outstanding Harrow XI at Lord's. He opened the innings with R. D. Walker, one of the famous Southgate brothers, and batted magnificently on a difficult wicket. He was a steady player who could also bowl useful roundarm of medium pace, and he fielded well.

In 1865, he was president of the Christchurch XI at Oxford, and ten years later, he was a member of the government, first as Parliamentary Secretary to the Board of Trade and then as Under Secretary at the India Office. Elected as MP first for Mid Lincs (1874-85), he then represented Horncastle (1885-93). The time for cricket diminished rapidly. In the words of *Cricket, A Weekly Record of the Game*: 'Until the cares of political life caused him to be troubled about many things, Mr Stanhope kept up an active interest in the game.'

The words have an ominous ring. When the Conservatives returned to office in 1885, he became first President of the Board of Education and then President of the Board of Trade in an administration which lasted barely seven months.

Gladstone's third ministry was even shorter, and Stanhope found himself back in government as Secretary of State for the Colonies at the beginning of August 1886. In January, the following year, he took up his last government post, Secretary of State for War. These positions were no sinecures, and Stanhope worked through troubled times. He reformed the administration of the army and established the Army Service Corps. He also adopted the magazine *Rifle*. His tenure of office ended in August 1892, and 16 months later, at the age of 53, he was dead.

The fall of Disraeli's Conservatives in April 1880, and the formation of Gladstone's second ministry did not totally rob the government of men with experience in first-class cricket. In January 1883, Gladstone appointed Henry Robert Brand as Surveyor General Ordnance.

Brand's political credentials were sound. He was the eldest son of the man who was a renowned Speaker of the House of Commons from 1872 to 1884. Henry Robert Brand succeeded to the title of Second Viscount Hampden in 1892, having previously been Liberal MP for Hertfordshire 1868-74.

His cricket background was less formidable. He was in the Rugby XI in 1858 and was regarded as 'a good and free hitter'. He played for Sussex against MCC at Lord's in 1860, and against Kent seven years later when he was a captain in the army. He made several appearances for the Gentlemen of Sussex, and for Hertfordshire; the two games for the Sussex County XI, seven years apart, were his only matches of importance. Sixteen runs at an average of 4.00 are not extraordinary figures but he was vice-president of the Sussex Club for some time.

His son, the Third Viscount Hampden, was in the Eton XI for three years, and his grandson, Hon David Francis Brand, played once for Cambridge University in 1922 and recommended by Lord Harris, went on the MCC tour of Australia and New Zealand the following winter. He was seen as a most promising all-rounder who had captained Eton well and made several good scores for the Eton Ramblers. Brand enjoyed a good tour, but he gave up first-class cricket on his return to England, leaving a career average of 15.37 with the bat from his 14 matches and 27 wickets at 28.03 with the ball. Thereafter he played mostly for Hertfordshire. He went into the City, served in Burma in the war, became chairman of the English, Scottish and Australian Bank, and succeeded to the title on the death of his brother in 1965.

The mention of Lord Harris brings us back to the 19th century and to the business of government. When Salisbury formed his first ministry in 1885 he retained the services of Hamilton, Hart Dyke and Stanhope as we have seen, and to his team he added two more cricketers, Lord Harris and Sir William Hood Walrond.

Walrond was a Conservative MP for 26 years, representing East Devonshire, 1880-85, and then Tiverton until 1905 when he became the First Baron Waleren of Uffcolme. He occupied successively the posts of Junior Lord of Treasury and Parliamentary Secretary to the Treasury before becoming Chancellor to the Duchy of Lancaster in 1902. He spent most of his time playing for Devon, his one first-class match being for MCC against Surrey in 1868 when he scored 13 not out and 13.

The career of Lord Harris in politics and cricket demands more of our attention. It was his great-grandfather, General Sir George Harris, who was raised to the peerage in recognition of his services in the American War of Independence and in India. His grandfather was also a soldier, seeing service in India, in western Europe during the

Napoleonic Wars, and at Waterloo where he was shot through the shoulder and forced to retire from the army. The Third Baron was not a soldier, but he made his way in public service, becoming successively Governor of Trinidad and of Madras.

While in Trinidad he married the daughter of the archdeacon of the island, the meeting of the two being helped in no small measure by the Attorney-General Charles Warner, the father of Pelham Warner. Ever the cricketing connection: George Robert Canning Harris was born at St Anne's, Trinidad, in February 1851.

He inherited the family love of the open air and of country sports, but, like his forebears, he was gifted with a high degree of physical and moral courage rather than with a strong intellect. He was autocratic in manner, fair in judgement and hot of temper. He could be a fearsome adversary in the council chamber and on the cricket field, as many found to their cost.

His passion for cricket was acquired in part from his father who was a member of MCC and a useful lob bowler. His mother died when he was two, but his travels round the world continued until his father returned to the family home at Belmont, near Faversham, in 1859. Alongside his public offices and services, the Third Baron was a director of a Kent railway company and a founder of Kent County Cricket Club.

For two years before going to Eton in 1864, the future Fourth Baron lived in London and received batting practice at Lord's as well as watching many of the matches of the day. He had no great innate ability but worked hard, and his passion for the game would not be denied. He won a place in the Eton XI in 1868 and captained the side in 1870, his last year. It was in this year, too, that he first played for Kent, making 8 in each innings in the match against MCC in August. He was to assist the county, when available, for the next 41 years. At the age of 19 he was a member of the committee, a precursor to his virtual control of the club for nearly 50 years.

Harris won his blue in his first year at Oxford, 1871, and he also played against Cambridge in 1872 and 1874, missing the 1873 game through injury. He led the side in 1874, and he was married shortly before the completion of his studies.

His life was full; his commitments many. In 1873, he was on his way to play for Lords and Commons against I Zingari when he was persuaded on the railway platform instead to go to Gravesend to play for Kent against Lancashire. By now, he had succeeded his father as the Fourth Lord Harris. In 1875, he became Kent's captain, and the same year he joined the committee of MCC From this point on, he was to justify *Wisden's* posthumous assessment of him: 'A great batsman and a brilliant field in his younger days, and all his life a commanding figure in the world of cricket.' He was to captain Kent until 1889 when his political duties forced him to stand down.

Harris had toured North America with Fitzgerald's team in 1872, and in 1878-79, he led a side of ten amateurs and two professionals to Australia. The Melbourne Club had originally asked I. D. Walker to take the side, but he was unable to make the trip, and Lord Harris was given the captaincy. He finished just behind Ulyett, the Yorkshire professional, in the batting averages for the tour.

One Test match was played, the third to be played between England and Australia, and the home side won with ease, but Harris scored 33 and 36. England lost their first seven wickets for 26 runs, but Harris and Absolom stopped a rout.

When Harris' side played New South Wales there were problems. There was heavy betting on the match. A run out decision caused crowd disturbance and a pitch invasion. His Lordship was struck by one of the invaders, strong diplomatic discussion took place, but the match was later completed. On leaving Australia, however, Lord Harris criticised the amateur umpires in the country and dismissed the idea that they were more honest than their professional counterparts. He also was emphatic that the betting element should be removed from Australian cricket.

The following year, 1880, the Australians toured England. The itinerary was late in being drawn up, and no match between the two countries was planned. Two attempts to set up a 'Test' match, the second by W. G. Grace, came to nothing, but C. W. Alcock, the Surrey secretary and one of the greatest men in sport in England, was more successful. He negotiated for a Test, the first in England, to be played at The Oval at the beginning of September. He worked energetically, and with considerable diplomatic skill, to bring the match about, but was aware he would need the support of Lord Harris if the game were to be played. Harris both gave his backing and led the side. He made 52, and England won by five wickets.

In 1884, he captained England on two more occasions, winning one match at Lord's, and drawing the other at The Oval. His rank and authority determined he should captain England in all four Test matches in which he appeared, but this should not be allowed to obscure the fact that he was also a very good batsman as a Test average of 29 shows.

Certainly, in 1884, he was supreme, scoring more runs than any other batsman in England, a remarkable feat in that Kent played the strongest counties in the country and were often faced with defeat. Harris was always at his best when faced with adversity. In Kent's second county match of the season, for example, they trailed Hampshire by 52 on the first innings and needed 243 to win on the last afternoon. Harris came in at 17-1 and hit 112 not out, including a six and eight fours, to lead his side to a seven-wicket victory. But this great season of 1884 was to be his last full season of first-class cricket although he was to remain captain of Kent until 1889.

Already, he had developed a reputation as a journalist on a variety of themes, most notably, of course, cricket, but also on agriculture, travel and politics. He was a major power in the government of cricket, referring to himself as a 'cricket socialist', one who had 'the interest of professional cricketers thoroughly at heart'. He fought against illegal bowling actions, as well as more controversially for county qualifications to be correctly and rigorously applied.

If Harris' position in the world of cricket was firmly established, his standing in the world of politics was growing daily. He was actively concerned with what was happening in Parliament and a member of major committees of the House of Lords. He was a founder of the Primrose League, which celebrated the beliefs of Disraeli and aimed to educate the masses politically in a move towards one nation. And in 1885, he became a member of the government.

Although his father had been an inactive Whig, Harris himself was a very active Conservative from his early days. It is generally accepted that he would have run for Parliament had he not been a member of the House of Lords where he was certainly a regular attender, active in legislation and debate. When the Conservatives came to power under Salisbury in June 1885, he was appointed Under Secretary of State for India. His immediate superior was Lord Randolph Churchill, a fellow Old Etonian. There were several in the new government who had played cricket for Eton.

The India Office was a vital arm of the government, but Harris' tenure of office was brief because the Conservatives fell in February 1886. Gladstone's third ministry was even briefer, for the First Home Rule Bill was defeated, and Salisbury and the Conservatives were back in power in July.

The Prime Minister now appointed Lord Harris as Under Secretary to the War Office where he served W. H. Smith. Smith may have lacked both ability and aspiration as a cricketer, but he owed much to cricketers in his political career. Harris knew the military mind, respected the army and thrived in the constant political and economic battles at the War Office.

His official duties prevented him from playing in more than a handful of matches each year, and, although he did not publicise the fact, he believed that 1889 would be his last season in first-class cricket which is why he relinquished the captaincy of Kent that year. In November 1889, it was announced that he was to be the new Governor of Bombay, an important and influential post.

There were challenges in India – social, economic, educational and hygienic. He attacked them robustly and saw cricket among all the classes as one means of solving several problems. Harris himself was both an ambassador and a leading player. He returned to England at the end of his tour of duty in the summer of 1895 and until December 1900, he was Lord in Waiting to Her Majesty Queen Victoria's Household. This was his last government appointment.

He had always been able to mix cricket and politics, but now he was able to concentrate more on the latter. He played for and captained a Kent XI which contained players not born when he first assisted the county. His return to the game was most welcomed by the spectators, but he could not escape controversy. He was one of those responsible for omitting Ranjitsinhji from the England team to play Australia at Lord's in 1896. Harris looked upon Ranji as a 'bird of passage' and believed that he should be doing something for cricket in India. He was also critical of Ranji's unique technique, believing that he was a bad model for young players taking to the game. 'Oh my Gooch and my Richards, yet to come, yet to come.'

Like many ex-politicians, Harris found his fortune rather depleted in a time of agricultural depression, and he pursued business interests in the city, but he was still able to use his powerful voice in the government of cricket, and, in July 1911, at Catford, he played the last of his 157 matches for Kent against the All-India touring team, scoring 36. At the age of 60 years 5 months, he was – and remains – the oldest man to appear in a first-class match in England. He was to continue playing good club cricket and scoring runs in his 60s and 70s, in fact most of his cricket was for Lords and Commons at that time. He was 73 when, as their captain, he saved the match against MCC by batting for an hour.

He continued to uphold what he saw as the integrity of cricket with a lofty idealism which often brought him into conflict with others, particularly on the question of qualification. In changing attitudes in a changing world after the First World War, he saw reds under the beds, and feared Bolshevism in cricket.

Nor were his tirades restricted to attacks on falling standards and law-breakers in cricket, for he spoke passionately in the House of Lords against the inclusion of a South African, Sir Benjamin Robinson, on the honours list in 1922. Robinson was branded as a crook by Harris due to his illicit financial dealings, and eventually he asked George V to remove his name from the list on which he was marked down for a peerage. Some would claim that Harris' part in exposing Robinson helped bring down Lloyd George's coalition government. This is hard to justify but it certainly played a part in putting an end to the sale of honours scandal of Maundy Gregory and his associates.

Lord Harris continued to fight for cricket, and for much else, active in the affairs of MCC, president and captain of Lords and Commons, until his death in 1932. He remained a colossus to the end. Not all were too sad to see him go, but then that is something of a compliment. In cricket and politics he could never be ignored.

Servers and
Keepers

IN THE pursuit of those who held high political office, we have been neglectful of others. The Honourable Joceline George Herbert Amherst really has the right to be amongst those who held high office. He had remarkable success as an all-rounder – steady bat; slow bowler – for Harrow against Eton in both 1864 and 1865. Harrow won both matches in which he played by an innings, and he hit 85 in the second match. In the first, he is said to have taken 8-69.

The problem is to identify the two first-class matches in which he played, for there is some doubt as to whether the Amherst who appeared for Gentlemen of Kent against Gentlemen of the MCC, at Canterbury in 1864, and for MCC against Hampshire, at Southampton, in 1866, was J. G. or his brother J. C.

It is certain that he went to Christ Church, Oxford, although he seems to have played no cricket at university, and that he was called to the Bar in 1874. The fifth son of William Pitt, he was private secretary to the Governor of Fiji from 1881 to 1883, and private secretary to the Governor of Western Australia from 1885 onwards. He was, until his sudden death in 1900 at the age of 53, a member of the Legislative Council of Western Australia.

If Amherst is somewhat peripheral to this chronicle, Sir Frederick Thomas Arthur Hervey-Bathurst is certainly closer to the centre. He was Member of Parliament for Wiltshire S. 1861-65 and played cricket for that county as well as for Devon. His pedigree for the game was a fine one, for his father, Sir Frederick Hutchinson played for Hampshire and regularly in Gentlemen v Players games (1831-54). A president of MCC, he was recognised as one of the great fast bowlers of his day as well as a noted 'slogger'. Frederick Thomas Arthur was also a renowned hitter, a good point fielder and a bowler of both fast round-arm or slow under-arm deliveries. He was in the Eton side for two seasons, 1849 and 1850, and he played for Hampshire three times in 1865 and 1866. He appeared in several other first-class matches in that period, but with limited success.

A Lieutenant-Colonel in the Grenadier Guards, Hervey-Bathurst fought in the Crimea War, for these were men of multi-talents and multi-interests for whom adventure and service were an integral part of life.

Henry Strutt did well for Harrow against Eton in 1859 when he hit 33 and twice stumped the great R. A. H. Mitchell who was to captain Oxford University three years in succession. This feat availed Strutt nothing when he went up to Cambridge. He played against MCC in 1862 and in the trial matches, but, in spite of his 31 not out at number ten against MCC, he did not get his blue. Indeed, that innings was to be the highest in the five first-class matches in which he played. He was described as 'a fine hitter, with fair defence; kept wicket well to slow bowling, but was not up to Lang's pace'. It must be remembered that wicketkeepers were expected to stand up to all bowlers at the time, whatever their pace.

He was a member of MCC and of Nottinghamshire County Cricket Club, becoming president of both clubs when he was in his 40s. Shortly after coming down from Cambridge, he travelled Europe with two friends, and, in December 1865, they were captured by brigands in

Greece. They were forced to pay £1,000 each in order to gain their release.

After this, the life of a Member of Parliament must have seemed dull. In 1868, Strutt was elected Liberal Member for East Derbyshire. He lost the seat in 1874, but in 1880 he was elected as Member for Berwick-on-Tweed, only to succeed to the title of Second Lord Belper later the same year.

Arthur Hugh Smith-Barry was another thwarted wicketkeeper. He did not make the XI at Eton or Oxford, and he played for Warwickshire before that county attained first-class status. He also assisted Cheshire and hit a century for them against Shropshire in 1864. His two first-class matches were for MCC, against Oxford University, with Lord Harris in the side, in 1873, and against Cambridge University two years later. He made 9 and 0 in the first match, and 3 and 2 in the second.

He became MP for Cork in 1867 and held the constituency until 1874. It was during this period that he represented the Gentlemen of Ireland, and it is interesting to note that I Zingari, for whom he played on many occasions, were persuaded to tour Ireland at the end of the 1873 season. The weather was dreadful, and, on a soggy pitch in Cork, I Zingari were bowled out for 35. The Cork slow bowlers exploited the conditions well, and they had excellent support in the field, with 'especially good work by their wicketkeeper'.

Smith-Barry became MP for South Huntingdonshire from 1886 to 1900. He was raised to the peerage in 1902, becoming the First Lord Barrymore.

This was the age, perhaps, when the talents of political wicketkeepers were not always recognised as they should have been. Wicketkeepers through the years, political or otherwise, have always argued that their craft has not been appreciated. James Round could certainly claim that his merits were not seen by judges of the game.

James Round is the first great name in the history of Essex cricket, but he did not appear in a first-class match for the county. It was he who chaired the meeting held at the Shire Hall, Chelmsford, on 14 January 1876, that brought the Essex County Cricket Club into existence. He was both chairman and captain of the club for the first six years of its existence, and he was treasurer until the beginning of 1883. It was his energy and enthusiasm which created Essex County Cricket Club, and, in 1894, he was to see them achieve first-class status, but by then his playing days were passed.

He was in the Eton XI of 1860, a strong side which included R. A. H. Mitchell and the Hon C. G. Lyttelton, and he was at that time regarded as a first-rate long-stop, a useful lob-bowler and a steady, painstaking batsman. A year after the Eton and Harrow match, Round was in the Gentlemen of Essex side that lost to the Gentlemen of Cambridge at Chelmsford.

He went up to Christ Church, Oxford, where he captained the college XI and developed into one of the finest amateur wicketkeepers of his day, or, as *Wisden* put it, 'one of the very best amateur wicketkeepers that ever asked: "How's that?" '

Incredibly, he was not given his blue at Oxford although, in 1864, while in residence, he played for Gentlemen against the Players at Lord's, coming in as a late replacement for an unwell R. A. H. Mitchell. He was to play on three more occasions for the Gentlemen, twice in 1867, when he had an outstanding game in The Oval fixture. In the Players' innings of 249, he caught three, stumped two, helped run out three batsmen and conceded only one bye.

A month before this match, Round had hit a ferocious 142 for Southgate against Oxford University on the Magdalen College Ground. He had now thrown off his earlier restraint as a batsman, and he appeared in many of the leading matches in 1867, including being in the England XI that beat Surrey and Sussex in Tom Lockyer's benefit match at The Oval.

His last appearance for the Gentlemen came at Lord's the following season, a match dominated by W. G. Grace who hit his first century in these famous matches and took ten wickets for 81 runs.

Round now played less and less first-class cricket, and his final appearance was for MCC against Nottinghamshire, at Lord's, in July 1869, although, as H. A. Richardson is credited with a stumping, it seems that he did not keep wicket. His final career figures are 22 matches with a batting average of 16.85 and 34 victims behind the stumps.

A tall, lithe man, Round's cricketing energies were now concentrated on his work for Essex and, as a player, for Lords and Commons Cricket in their occasional matches, playing alongside Strutt in the first game the parliamentarians ventured against Harrow School. In 1868, Round had become a barrister, and the same year, when Gladstone formed his first ministry, he was elected as member for East Essex and Harwich in the Conservative interest.

Although serving on the MCC committee and helping to bring Essex into being, he became Assistant Private Secretary to Sir Michael Hicks-Beach, the Chief Secretary for Ireland when Disraeli shuffled his government in April 1878. Round survived all the elections he fought even when constituencies were altered and he represented North East Essex.

He saw out the ministries of Gladstone, Disraeli, Salisbury and Balfour, and when he stood down after the resignation of the government in December 1905, he had been a Conservative Member of Parliament for 38 years. This should have earned him a place in *Wisden's* record section, let alone his achievements on the cricket field and his pioneering for Essex.

Was there, in those later years of Victoria's reign, some mystic link between the art of wicket-keeping and the skill of the politician which, as yet, remains unexplained? We have spoken of Round, Smith-Barry and Strutt, and now we must turn our attention to William Nicholson, Harrow, Middlesex and MCC, Liberal and Conservative.

William Nicholson was one of the very few presidents of MCC in the 19th century who was not born into the aristocracy. When he became president in 1879 he was only the second since 1845 not to have a title. His wealth – and there was much of it, for when he died in 1908 he left £621,162; only three first-class cricketers have left more – came from the distilling and selling of a famous brand of gin.

He was born in 1824, and, commencing in 1841, he was in the

Harrow XI for three years, captaining the side in his last season when, it was said, with 'his strict management and fine play, he helped much to win both against Winchester and Eton'. He scored his runs very quickly, adopting the maxim that attack was the best form of defence, was very fast between the wickets, an excellent judge of a run, and 'one of the best wicketkeepers in England, standing up pluckily to the fastest bowling', receiving 'many a severe blow' in the process.

He played for the Gentlemen of England in 1845 and for the Gentlemen against the Players in every one of the Lord's contests from 1846 until 1858. He was an active participator in Canterbury Week as a member of the old and celebrated Clapton club, an early member of I Zingari and a keen Old Stager. He played for Middlesex sides before the county club came into being, and for county club itself against MCC in its first season, 1864, and against Hampshire the following year. That was his last appearance for the county which he had helped to establish and which his generosity was to help survive.

By the time Middlesex were a county club, Nicholson was at the veteran stage, but he had been a formidable opponent in the 1850s. In 1852, he appeared not only for the Gentlemen, but for MCC, Gentlemen of the South, Gentlemen of England, and for England against Kent. Against Kent, at Lord's, he made the two highest scores of the match, 39 and 70. This second innings brought his side victory by seven wickets, which, as they had needed 156 to win, was an outstanding achievement at this period.

He did not keep wicket in this match, but it is estimated that in 148 matches of importance between 1850 and 1865, he caught 110 and stumped 89 batsmen. He also hit 3,447 runs, average 13.78, on wickets upon which, today, many players would scorn to park their cars.

Yet it is not for his achievements on the field that Nicholson is best remembered. He became a member of MCC in 1845, and, 21 years later, with the Lord's ground under threat from developers, he lent the club money to purchase the freehold at an interest of five per cent. He became a trustee, and, as we have noted, president in 1879. In 1889, the club turned to him again when they wanted to build a new pavilion.

There was always a reluctance on the part of some of the hierarchy of MCC to ask Nicholson, for they saw him as something akin to nouveau riche, but sense prevailed. As Tony Lewis points out in his history of the old club, of the £26,000 liabilities that the MCC had in 1899, £6,000 was owed to William Nicholson. By 1904, the club was solvent. Like William Ward before him, Nicholson had saved and helped to develop Lord's.

Nicholson took a big gamble when he lent MCC in 1866, for Marsden, who owned the freehold of the ground, wanted more than £18,000 for it, and Nicholson must have provided the bulk with little guarantee he would ever get his money back. The club's administrators had not been noted for their business sense or their foresight; the committee could have bought the freehold for £7,000 in 1860.

Nicholson's loan was particularly brave as he was venturing into politics at the time. In the General Election of 1866, he won the seat of Petersfield in Hampshire for the Liberals, the party which seemed most to represent the interests of tradesmen like himself. He held it until 1874 when he was ousted in the election which swept Disraeli back to power.

In 1880, he contested the seat again, perhaps because of the Liberal Licensing Act this time as a Conservative, and, in spite of the fact that the Liberals were returned nationally, he won the ballot. He held the seat until January 1886, when he suffered from one of the very few Conservative splits. He was opposed by an unofficial Tory candidate, who polled only 179 votes. It was enough, however, to give victory to the Liberal who beat Nicholson by 161 votes.

That was the end of his political career. Nicholson lived until the age of 85, a man of great vigour with a shrewd business sense, a feel for adventure and a hint of sentimentality. He led a busy life, but he remembered long and was trusting. In 1893, he bought a large plot of land at Harrow and presented it to his old school.

Principally, however, he was a benefactor to Middlesex County Cricket Club and, above all, to MCC. It is doubtful whether Lord's or the club would have survived without his assistance.

There were wicketkeepers who served in important political positions without the necessity of fighting an election – for example, Sir Courtenay Edmund Boyle who played in two dozen first-class matches between 1865 and 1872. He was of Irish descent and born in Jamaica where his father, an army officer, was stationed. At Charterhouse, he was soon revealed as an outstanding classical scholar as well as captain of the cricket XI.

At Christ Church, Oxford, he was noted for his extraordinary memory for quotations, but his interest in outside activities outweighed his concern for study, and, academically, he was a disappointment. Sportingly, he thrived.

He was a good racquets player, was tennis champion of the university in 1866 and 1867, and beat the Cambridge champion in both years. He won his blue at cricket in all three years, 1865 to 1867, being described as a 'useful bat' and 'an excellent wicketkeeper', although, as was the custom of the age, he did not keep wicket all the time.

He played for Northamptonshire and for Buckinghamshire, neither of whom was first-class, and appeared in MCC sides, mostly against the universities, alongside W. G. Grace. His last game of note was for MCC against his old university in 1872. MCC won by an innings, but Boyle was out for 0, and he does not seem to have kept wicket. His 24 first-class matches yielded an average of 14.02 and 27 caught or stumped.

By then, public service and work were in his mind. He was related to Lord Spencer, Viceroy of Ireland in Gladstone's First Administration, 1868 to 1874, and Spencer took Boyle to Dublin on his staff, first as Assistant Private Secretary, and then as Private Secretary.

In 1873, he became Inspector of English Local Government, and three years later, Inspector of Eastern Counties. With Gladstone back in power, he retained the inspectorates, and he went back to Dublin with Spencer. In May 1882, he was one of the first on the scene after the murders of Cavendish and Burke in Phoenix Park.

Boyle returned to England, became a Companion of the Order of Bath, Assistant Secretary to the Local Government Board, and then

Assistant Secretary to the Board of Trade. He was concerned with railway revisions and the introduction of electric light. He was knighted and became Permanent Secretary to the Board of Trade.

In spite of these arduous public duties, he remained a sportsman until his death in 1901. He was an after-dinner speaker of repute and a keen fisherman. It was he who was responsible for the Royal Commission on Salmon Fishing Laws. Nor was he lost to cricket, for, on his death, *The Times* revealed that he had been 'Old Blue' who had been writing in their columns advocating cricket reform and causing so much heated debate. Traditional civil service anonymity!

Few men, it seems, have been able to combine the qualities needed to enable one to crouch behind the stumps permanently keen and receptive with the qualities needed to sit in the House of Commons or House of Lords permanently keen and receptive. Inevitably, the art of keeping wicket has had to give way to the problems of government. So it was with Robert Threshie Reid whose prowess was too soon forgotten.

Born in Corfu, still a modest cricket centre, educated at Cheltenham College, he gained renown both as a scholar and an athlete. He was the best racquets player in the school, was in the cricket XI for three years and became Head of School. He was given a place at Magdalen, but threw it up and won a scholarship to Balliol. His career at Oxford was outstanding, and it was said of him: 'Few better all round men have passed through the university.'

Apart from his academic achievements, he was regarded as a fair short distance runner and as a wicketkeeper of the front rank. In 1865, he played for the university against Southgate and, twice, against MCC, but he did not get his blue as a freshman. He was in the side for the Varsity match in the next three years, however, and played alongside Boyle and Maitland, whom we shall meet later.

In four years, he played 15 times for Oxford, but that was the extent of his first-class cricket. He caught 17 and stumped five, and when one considers that he often shared the duty behind the stumps, that is no mean achievement. He caught three and stumped one in the Varsity match of 1867 when Cambridge won by five wickets, but his career ended strangely the following season when he was marked as absent in Oxford's second innings. Later hands have added (hurt), but there is no proof of this. Whatever the cause, he was to be lost to the cricket field at the age of 22.

He was from a family who had specialised in the law, and therefore prepared himself for the Bar. In 1871, he was called by the Inner Temple, and, appropriately, was assigned to the Oxford circuit. In his new position he gave one of the first indications of his total commitment to the new Liberalism by breaking with the convention that barristers should travel first-class. He refused to do so, saying that it was not necessary and that, in any case, he could not afford such a luxury.

He had a rapid rise in the legal profession, but now his interest in politics, and his ideals began to assert themselves. In April 1880, Gladstone was swept back to power, and Reid was elected as the second Liberal Member for Hereford. Two years later, he took silk, but his legal reputation faded a little as his loyal and ardent support of Gladstone grew.

After the Redistribution Bill of 1885, Hereford became a single member constituency, and Reid had to look for another seat. In December 1885, he stood for Dumbartonshire and lost. There were, however, divisions within the Liberal Party over the question of Home Rule for Ireland, and, in June 1886, Gladstone's Liberals were decisively beaten at the polls. Reid was an outspoken and fervent supporter of Gladstone and his policies, yet he won the seat at Dumfries, and he held it until 1906 after which he came the First Earl of Loreburn.

In the Gladstone, later Rosebery, administration, he was first Solicitor General, briefly, and then Attorney General. A man of vigorous independence, he was called as arbitrator in the boundary dispute between British Guiana and Venezuela in 1899. He also supported the Boers in their quarrels with the British, making himself unpopular both politically and professionally, but he was a man of the utmost integrity as was to be proved when, following the large Liberal majority in 1906, he was appointed Lord Chancellor. One of his principal achievements in this post was to establish the Court of Criminal Appeal, a task achieved not without strong opposition from his own profession.

Harder battles lay ahead. He presided over the House of Lords during a most difficult period. In 1909, the Lords rejected Lloyd George's budget, and Reid, now Loreburn, had to steer the path through a constitutional crisis. The Liberals won elections in both January and December 1910. The Parliament Act was passed the following year, and the power of the elected members was strengthened.

Loreburn conducted himself throughout this period with an inflexible integrity that left him a solitary figure. There were those in his own party who criticised him for not showing bias towards the Liberals. He felt it his duty to uphold the law and the constitution, and, in the end, he was proved correct, but the struggle and the criticism took their toll of him. He resigned in 1911 and retired to Dover where he wrote and continued the interest in sport which had never left him.

In 1907, he was president of MCC and of Kent, and, in January 1905, *Vanity Fair* published a cartoon of him by Spy (Leslie Ward), captioned 'Mr Attorney, reference Statesmen 646'. He found no place among the cricketers, his death went unremarked in *The Cricketer*, and gets no mention in *Double Century*, the history of MCC, but in his youth he had been considered a wicketkeeper of the front rank. He gave his life to politics, and it left him bruised, tired and sick. Happier, perhaps, if he had remained crouched behind the stumps but not in overall achievement.

House Full

IN THE latter part of the 19th century, and in the early years of the 20th century, some 50 members sat in the House of Commons who could claim to have played first-class cricket. It must be admitted that the first-class credentials of one or two are less substantial than those of others, but to have appeared in one match that has been accorded first-class status is an honour many sitting in the House today would covet.

John Heron Maxwell-Heron, for example, was the Liberal Member for Kirkcudbright from 1880 until 1885, and, at Islington, in 1865, he appeared as Captain Maxwell for the Gentlemen of England against the Gentlemen of Middlesex. He scored three and took two wickets with his left-hand round-arm bowling.

Then there was Thomas Keay Tapling who was educated at both Harrow and Brighton, but, as a hard-hitting middle-order batsman, was not asked to play in a match while up at Cambridge. He did appear for MCC against the university in 1886 and scored 5 and 0. This was his only first-class appearance although he did tour Ceylon and India with G. F. Vernon's team in 1889-90. This was the first tour by a party of English players to the Indian sub-continent, but only three of the side were appearing regularly in county matches at that time.

Tapling was Conservative MP for the Harborough Division of Leicester from 1886 until his death in April 1891, at the age of 36.

As with many of us, the desire was greater than the performance in many of these noble men. Viscount William Heneage Legge Lewisham, who became the Sixth Earl of Dartmouth in 1891, in the words of *Wisden*, 'played cricket with much enthusiasm, but did not succeed in getting into either the Eton or Oxford XI'. He was president of Kent, of MCC, in 1893, and of Staffordshire for 40 years. He played for both Staffordshire and Shropshire, and he was a fervent supporter of I Zingari and of Lords and Commons Cricket. He was the Member for West Kent from 1878-85, and for Lewisham from 1885-91.

Lewisham was a trustee of MCC and served on the committee alongside the benefactor, Nicholson. His son was to become president of MCC at the time of the body-line crisis and to have a hard time during his term of office. In spite of these close connections with the game and his undying passion for it, Viscount Lewisham appeared in only one first-class match when, three days before his 26th birthday, in 1877, he was in the MCC X1 against Hampshire for the opening match of the season at Lord's. Batting at number nine, he was not out five in the first innings. Hampshire were forced to follow on, and, eventually, MCC needed 55 to win. Anstruther was out for 0, but Russell and Lewisham hit off the runs. Lewisham finished unbeaten on 24 so that he can claim to be one of the very few cricketers never to have been dismissed during his first-class career.

Beilby Lawley, who succeeded to the title of Third Lord Wenlock in 1880, can claim no such honour, but, like Lewisham, he was one whose enthusiasm was not matched by his ability. He could find no place in the XIs at either Eton or Cambridge, but he was a member of MCC from 1870 until his death in 1912, and he was president of the Club in 1885 when he chaired a committee which brought in severe reorganisation of MCC Among the changes they suggested were that the secretary should live in close proximity to the ground, that records of scores of club matches should be printed at the MCC's printing plant, not written in manuscript, and that the payment to score-card sellers of an half-penny per card sold was excessive.

Beilby, who was MP for Chester from April to July 1880, was always to be more remembered for his contributions to the administration and legalities of the game than for his prowess on the field. He was a close friend of Lord Harris, and Governor of Madras at the time that Harris was Governor of Bombay. The two often opened the innings together in matches for Ganeshkhind whose ground Harris had established. Harris valued Wenlock's opinion and judgement, and Wenlock was one of the three to pass sentence on the bowling action of Sir William Coote Hedley in 1900. Hedley was asked to stand down from the Kent side although he later made appearances for Hampshire and Somerset.

In spite of having the reputation and power as an authority on the game, Beilby Lawley enjoyed no distinguished first-class career. His one appearance in a match now recognised as first-class was for I Zingari against Yorkshire at Scarborough in 1880, a few weeks after he had been unseated at Chester. He batted number ten, was stumped off Peate for three, did not bowl but caught the redoubtable Ephrain Lockwood. I Zingari won by three wickets thanks to fine batting from Ivo Bligh.

Frank Hardcastle, MP for the Westhoughton Division of Lancashire from 1885 to 1892, played twice for Lancashire in 1869, when he was in his mid-20s. He appeared against MCC and Surrey but managed only 17 runs in four innings and probably decided to concentrate on politics.

Few men were able to meet the demands of politics and first-class cricket at one and the same time. The life of William Fuller-Maitland, for example, was well compartmentalised, but he appeared in 38 first-class matches in a comparatively short period (1864-67) at a time when few sides engaged in more than half-a-dozen games in a season.

He was born at Stansted and was to play in non-first-class cricket for both Essex and Oxfordshire. He had a prodigious talent, for he was in the Harrow XI for four years before going up to Oxford and getting his blue as a Freshman in 1864. He had match figures of 8-53 in the Varsity match and shared in the partnership with R. A. H. Mitchell which won the match for Oxford by four wickets.

In his second Varsity match, he took 8-76, batted well, and Oxford again won. Although he took fewer wickets in 1866 and 1867, he played innings of 51 and 45. He captained the side in his last year without any marked success. He had not developed his bowling until the end of his days at Harrow, but so good was he that he won a place in the Gentlemen's side while still in his first year at Oxford and was a regular against the Players until 1869.

Fuller-Maitland bowled very slowly with total command of flight and length, and he turned his leg-breaks to such an extent that he had no equal in his day. In the Varsity match of 1867, he pitched a ball outside leg stump so wide that the batsman, J. S. E. Hood, offered no shot, only to find that the ball turned back sharply and bowled him. Shades of Shane Warne's opening ball to Michael Gatting at Old Trafford in 1993!

Rarely did he fail with the ball although James Round's 142 for Southgate in 1867 was made against him. He finally had Round caught. He troubled all batsmen, fielded magnificently to his own bowling and played many fine innings. As time progressed, he bowled less, and, in his last match, for MCC against Yorkshire in 1870, he did not bowl at all. To lesser mortals, he was one of those infuriating men who possessed so immense a talent that it mattered little to him.

In passing, it should be mentioned that Fuller-Maitland represented Oxford in both the high jump and the long jump in the university sports, and that he appeared for Oxford at racquets in both the singles and doubles. There were many who felt that Oxford had never seen a better sportsman, certainly no better spin bowler.

He was only 26 when he played his last first-class cricket match, and his neglect of the game was lamented by all who admired him. Later in life, he gave the reasons for his leaving the game. One was that, like Norman Mitchell-Innes of Somerset and England in years to come, he suffered very badly from hay fever in June and July. The second, and more significant reason, was Fuller-Maitland's desire to travel. He went to India, Spain and America, and, finding he was untroubled by hay fever in these countries, he lived in each for a while.

Once his travels were at an end, he contemplated a political career.

He was elected Member of Parliament for Breconshire in 1875 when he was 31, and he remained in the seat until he decided to retire 19 years later. He died at the age of 88, in 1932, at which time he was the oldest surviving Oxford blue.

Denzil Onslow was in Parliament for half the period of Fuller-Maitland's term. He was elected to represent Guildford as a Conservative in 1874, but after the Third Reform Act ten years later, Guildford was disenfranchised. His first-class cricket was over a year before he went into Parliament, but he also played in India where he had been born and where he was Finance Secretary to three successive Finance Ministers. He appeared for Simla and Calcutta, and his service in India restricted his appearances for Sussex – he was educated at Brighton College and had a residence in the town – to six which were spread over a period of nine years.

An attacking middle-order batsman and quick bowler, Onslow had done reasonably well in the two Varsity matches for Cambridge, 1860 and 1861, and he was later to show his worth, both for MCC and for Sussex, against the strong Surrey side of the period. His first-class career was, however, hardly impressive – an average of ten in 23 matches and 20 wickets with the ball.

In spite of the fact that he played for Sussex, Onslow was to serve on the Surrey Committee for a quarter of a century and to work hard for that club. His grandfather had played for many years earlier and had also represented Kent and Hampshire sides in the days before birth or residential qualifications were seriously considered.

It is strange how so many of the lives of these cricketing politicians cross and intermingle and follow similar patterns. Like Onslow, William Stanley Kenyon-Slaney was born in India where his father served in the East India Company's Army. Kenyon-Slaney was in the I Zingari side which beat Yorkshire at Scarborough in 1880, Beilby Lawley's only first-class match. Like Lewisham, Kenyon-Slaney did not appear in the XI at Oxford, and like Tapling, he first entered Parliament in 1886.

He was a limited cricketer, a right-handed batsman noted most for his fielding at cover point, and he could find no place in the side at Eton. He was reputed to be a fair scholar, but an enthusiastic footballer and cricketer. Certainly, at soccer, he won honours, and he did much to popularise the game.

Having already matriculated, he spent only one year at Christ Church, Oxford, 1866-67. He took a commission in the Household Brigade, and it was for his regiment, for I Zingari and for MCC that most of his cricket was played. He appeared in some 11 matches (1869-80) now looked upon as first-class, hitting 145 runs. He was on the committee of MCC for eight years, and also served on the committee of the old Prince's Club.

Kenyon-Slaney – the Slaney was added in deference to his mother's family from whom a large estate in Shropshire was inherited – was something of an impetuous, joyful cricketer, enthusiastic in all that he did. He had played for Eton at soccer, and, in 1876, appeared for Old Etonians in the FA Cup Final. Three years earlier, he had played centre-forward for England against Scotland at The Oval, the second international match between the two countries, and the first to be played in England. According to *Bell's Life*, 'For England Captain Kenyon-Slaney was of the greatest service'. In fact, he opened the scoring when he shot home following a throw-in, and he repeated the feat close to the end of the game to give England a 4-2 victory after they had been 2-1 down.

He fought with the Grenadier Guards in the Egyptian War, and he was Colonel of the Regiment by 1887. He retired from the army in 1892, but by that time he was already a Member of Parliament. As Conservative and Unionist candidate he had contested the Wellington Division of Shropshire in 1885, but was defeated. A year later, he stood for the Newport Division of Shropshire with more success. He was to remain the Member for that constituency until his death in 1908. Twice he was victorious at the polls; twice he was returned unopposed.

Cricket and sport in general still pulsated through his life. Elected in July 1886, he made his maiden speech in the House of Commons some five weeks later when he urged that there should be a recreation ground for the garrison of the metropolis. The result was the Guards' cricket ground at Burton's Court, Chelsea.

Memorably, in November 1890, he moved the address in reply to the Queen's Speech and set a precedent by confining himself to a single sentence of thanks. Would that more politicians had followed his example! In fact, he spoke often in the House. He was an ardent tariff reformer, and, true cricketer again, introduced a Bill on pure beer. As on the sports field, so in Parliament, there was a zest in all that he did.

In Shropshire, he was regarded as a model landlord. He ensured that every cottage on his estate had three bedrooms, proper drainage and a good water supply. Active to the last, Kenyon-Slaney died of pneumonia at his home in Shropshire in 1908. It was for Shropshire that he had played his only county cricket – 11 matches to average 10.35 with the bat.

Like Kenyon-Slaney, Arthur Frederick Jeffreys could find no place in the XI at either Eton or Oxford, which was something of a surprise as he was considered a good right-handed batsman. He marked his first appearance at Lord's with an innings of 92 for MCC and Ground against Rugby School, in 1871. His first-class debut came for MCC against his old university the following season, and, while in Australia early in 1873, he played for New South Wales in the annual match against Victoria at the Albert Ground, Sydney.

He played with some regularity for MCC, and, in 1876, he made his debut for Hampshire. He appeared in all four of the county's fixtures that season and hit 42 in the match against Kent when Lord Harris' side was beaten by an innings. He scored 51 in the opening game of the following season when Hampshire were beaten by MCC, but thereafter business and politics began to claim him, and his last first-class game was for MCC in 1879. An average of 14.31 from 26 matches is his record.

He entered Parliament as the Conservative Member for the Northern Division of Hampshire in 1887, and in June 1905, Balfour appointed him Parliamentary Secretary to the Treasury. Sadly, his period in office was short, for the government fell in December. He died two months later at the age of 57.

Representing one's county was a somewhat casual affair for amateurs until the last decade of the 19th century by which time the County Championship had really begun to take shape. Joseph Leese, for example, was in the first all Lancashire match played by the newly-formed Lancashire County Cricket Club, at Old Trafford, in July 1865.

The game was against Middlesex for whom Vyell Walker took all ten Lancashire wickets in the second innings, but the home county won by 62 runs. J. F. Leese, a hard-hitting batsman, scored 33 and 0, and was, at the time, among Lancashire's leading amateurs. He was also a good fielder at point.

A Mancunian, Leese was barely 19 at the time of his Lancashire debut, but his 24 matches for the county were to stretch until 1881 by which time he was 36. He played only once in that last season in which Lancashire were unquestionably the leading county, winning ten and drawing three of their 13 matches. His brother Ernest played for Lancashire and there were three sons and a nephew all of whom were to appear in first-class cricket.

Certainly, J. F. Leese could have appeared for Lancashire more if business, time and inclination had allowed, but he often preferred to play for the Gentlemen of the North rather than for the county. *Wisden* recalled that his major feats were in minor matches, 72 for the Gentlemen of Lancashire against the Gentlemen of Yorkshire, and 62 for Eighteen Veterans against MCC in the Centenary Match of 1887. Since he was only 39 at the time of this last innings, he seems rather a young veteran.

It was five years after this innings that he became Liberal Member of Parliament for Accrington. He had followed a career as a successful barrister, and remained in the House of Commons until 1909. Created a baronet he retired to a cottage in Guildford. There was no indication that he maintained an interest in cricket, and he was not among the most active of MCC members, nor does he find a place in the annals of Lords and Commons Cricket.

In contrast, the name of John Maunsell Richardson is to be found in many records of the 19th century, particularly the sporting ones.

Indeed, he is another of those men gifted with so much talent as to become the envy of others. He was in the Harrow XI for two years, and on both occasions, the match against Eton was won by an innings.

He gained his blue in each of his three years at Cambridge, 1866 to 1868, and Boyle, whom he caught in his second match, and 'Bob' Reid, Lord Loreburn, were among his opponents.

As well as being proficient at cricket, Richardson was outstanding at the long jump, racquets, the hurdles and fencing. As he was also a huntsman and a jockey without peer, it is, perhaps, true to say that he was at least as great an all-round sportsman as C. B. Fry, or could have been had he pursued his remarkable abilities to the full.

Sixteen of his 18 first-class matches were played while he was at Cambridge, and his last game was for MCC in 1874. His father-in-law and his brother both played for Harrow, but John Richardson played little cricket after he left university. He appeared for Lincolnshire, his home county, and for Cheshire, and there were games for teams like I Zingari, Quidnuncs and Na Shuler. Once he hit 188 for the Jockeys against the Press, but his passing from the game at the top level was to be lamented.

He was credited with having anticipated the glide, a shot which was later to become an integral part of the repertoire of all leading batsmen. In *Scores and Biographies*, Haygarth despaired that Richardson 'is an excellent batsman, a splendid field, generally at a distance from the wicket, and can bowl slow round-arm well. He promised to turn out a first-rate cricketer, had he only continued the game.' But there were other things in Richardson's life, notably horses and his Lincolnshire estate.

We have stated that he was a noted huntsman, and we should now consider his achievements as a jockey, for the description of his being the greatest amateur jockey of the age was not come by lightly. He became associated with one, Captain James Machell. Machell had been an officer in the West Yorkshire Regiment with a passion for horse-racing. He had a particular party-trick for which he was noted in the Officers' Mess in that he could jump on to the mantlepiece from a standing start. He resigned his commission in 1863 when he was refused leave to attend the Doncaster Races.

Machell staked his all on the one horse he owned, Bacchus, and he won £10,000 at Newmarket. With this money, he set up as a trainer, a dealer and a gambler. He was an excellent judge, and he teamed up with Richardson whom he asked to ride his horse, Disturbance, in the Grand National of 1873. Originally, there were 108 entries for the race, but eventually 28 ran. Richardson was a natural horseman and a trainer who recognised the qualities and capabilities not only of the horse he was riding but also of those he was riding against.

The 1873 Grand National was run on a glorious day, and it seemed that the second favourite, Ryshworth, would win with ease as he was leading and comfortable until the last flight. Disturbance had been at the back, but Richardson brought him gently to the front and drew level with Ryshworth at the last jump, beating him with ease on the run-in. Disturbance was a 20-1 outsider, and Richardson's handling of the horse won the highest possible praise.

Captain Machell had three horses in the Grand National the following year – Disturbance, Defence and Reugny. With 12st 9lbs, Disturbance had been weighed out of contention, and Defence was in receipt of only 10lbs, so Machell asked Richardson to ride the French-bred Reugny. Richardson agreed to do so.

With supreme confidence in his jockey, Machell hoped to make a great deal of money if Reugny won the National, but he learned that Lincolnshire farming friends of Richardson's had secured the best prices about Reugny, and he exploded with rage when he realised that 5-1 were now the only odds available. He confronted Richardson and accused him of cheating by giving information to his friends. Outraged and disgusted at the accusation, Richardson threatened to withdraw from the engagement to ride Reugny. He was persuaded to relent, but he vowed that this would be the last race.

There was one false start to the 1874 Grand National. When, finally, they were off, Reugny came from behind to win by six lengths. Richardson rode a marvellous race, and the critics were unanimous in their praise that he alone could have won on Reugny that day. But Richardson kept his word; he never rode in a race again. Captain Machell's meteoric success on the turf provided him with sufficient funds to re-acquire his family estate in Westmorland. But he lost Richmond forever.

Clean-shaven and handsome, in appearance John Richardson was ahead of his time. In sporting ability, he was in a class of his own, and he was to add political credentials to his sporting ones. In 1894 and 1895, he was Conservative MP for Brigg in the county of his beloved Lincolnshire.

He died in 1912. One wonders what he might have achieved had he played more cricket, ridden in more Grand Nationals or even continued to run and jump. One thing is certain. There are not too many Members of Parliament over the years who have played first-class cricket and ridden a Grand National winner.

The Golden Age

IT HAS not been easy to determine how much first-class cricket a man played before the 1860s and harder still to assess his worth as a politician. With the start of cricket's Golden Age it all becomes easier.

Linked often with the name of Lord Harris, for example, is that other pillar of the cricket establishment, Lord Hawke who, like J. M. Richardson, came from Lincolnshire. Hawke's achievements for Yorkshire and his efforts on behalf of the professional cricketer are as well known as the misrepresentation of his remarks on professionals captaining England. Nothing is said of his political activities except that, like Lord Harris, he was a Conservative, and that he was in the House of Lords for 50 years. He should speak for himself:

'I first took my seat in the House of Lords in 1888, and though I have never spoken, I have been pretty regular in my attendance whenever I have been in London during the Session. When Rosebery drew up his list of 400 selected peers who should have seats in a reformed House of Lords, he did me the honour to include me in it.

'I detest making a speech. To do so is a matter of conscientious labour on my part previously, for I always write out and prepare with great care what I have to say. But I am very fond of listening to good speeches. Anybody can get up and talk with a volume of notes in his hands. It is quite another thing to speak with ease with your hands behind your back. The greatest orator I ever heard was the old Duke of Argyll.

'It is a very easy post to preside over the House of Lords, for everything is decorous, and in a big debate the order of going to speak is settled beforehand. I have never in my life dined at the House of Lords, but I remember going back one night because I wanted to hear Lord Curzon, and about nine finding some poor devil who had inherited his coronet talking to absolutely empty benches. That is the sort of verbal tragedy which demands either an epic or the type of liquid restorative not approved of by Lady Astor.'

The placid and decorous House of Lords which Lord Hawke describes is difficult to reconcile with the House that 'Bob' Reid, the Lord Chancellor, endured in Edwardian times which came close to destroying his health and which sparked the Parliament Act of 1911. Hawke was more at home at Lord's than in the House of Lords.

If the Edwardian Age was a Golden Age for cricket, it was also a golden age for the cricketing politician, for some two dozen first-class cricketers stalked the corridors of power in the first decade of the 20th century. To begin with there were the Heath brothers.

Sir James appeared in only one first-class match, for MCC against Derbyshire in 1882 when he scored 16. He also played for Staffordshire, and he was Conservative MP for North West Staffordshire from 1892 to 1906.

His younger brother, Arthur Howard Heath, enjoyed a more spectacular sporting career. A middle-order right-handed batsman and a fast round-arm or lob bowler, A. H. Heath was in the Clifton XI for three years and scored two impressive centuries during his time at the College. Very strong on the off side, he appeared in six matches for Gloucestershire before going up to Oxford. As that side was invariably chosen by W. G. Grace, the schoolboy must have impressed the great man, especially in his eagerness to hit the ball.

Heath was in the University XI in each of his four seasons at Oxford, but he never really did himself justice in the Varsity matches although scoring runs against the counties. He played two matches for Middlesex while he was in his third year at Oxford, but Staffordshire was his home and his county, and he assisted them from 1879 to 1898, captaining the side between 1884 and 1893. He was also both secretary and treasurer of the county club for long periods.

He could score at a quick rate; at Stoke in 1889 he hit 217 in four hours against Lincolnshire. *Wisden* was to remark with some humour on his occasional bowling, recalling when he bowled for MCC against Surrey. The match was at Lord's some ten days after the Varsity match of 1876. Heath bowled only in the second innings, taking 1-13 in five overs, but sending down three wides and a no-ball which, at that time, did not count against the bowler. The over in which he took his wicket began with a wide, the second jumped over long-stop's head and resulted in five byes, the third knocked Elliott's middle stump out of the ground, and the fourth all but bowled Humphrey. The fifth ball was a wide which produced two runs, and the last ball of what should have been a four-ball over was the only uneventful delivery.

To single out this particular over is rather unfair on Heath who did take 26 first-class wickets in the 44 matches in which he played between 1875 and 1894. He also hit 969 runs.

As well as gaining his 'blue' for cricket Heath also represented the university in the four Varsity rugby matches (1876-79) played when he was in residence. Blues were not awarded for rugby until 1882, but Heath remains one of the very few men to have played in four rugby matches for Oxford against Cambridge. He also played for England against Scotland at The Oval in 1876. England won by a goal and a try to nil, on what was the last occasion when an international rugby match was 19-a-side.

With all his sporting achievements behind him, Colonel Heath, a regular army officer, entered politics. He was Conservative Member of Parliament for Hanley from 1900 to 1906, and for Leek in 1910.

So, the Heath brothers were both first-class cricketers, and they were both Members of Parliament, but if we are now concerned with brotherhoods, it is time we considered the Lytteltons.

The Fourth Lord Lyttelton was the first man to feature in this chronicle. As we indicated, he was not among the foremost of cricketers, although he did play once for Cambridge University. What was remarkable about him was that he had six sons who appeared in first-class cricket. They were Charles George, who won his blue in each of his four years at Cambridge; George William Spencer; Arthur Temple; Robert Henry; Edward, who became Headmaster of Eton; and Alfred of whom we shall hear much more shortly.

Charles George Lyttelton, who became the Eighth Viscount Cobham in 1889, was educated at Eton where he was in the XI from 1857 to 1860 and was captain in his last two years. He did not do himself justice in the Varsity match, but he topped the Cambridge batting averages in both 1863 and 1864. He hit 101 against Surrey at The Oval in the first of those seasons, and 128 against MCC at Fenner's in the second when he averaged a remarkable 34.42 in all matches for the season. He was also a good right-arm under-hand bowler at that time and could keep wicket, but he lost interest in bowling because of back trouble.

There were those, Maitland among them, who put C. G. Lyttelton on a par with E. M. Grace and R. A. H. Mitchell as the greatest batsmen of the day. He was a regular member of the Gentlemen's team against the Players from his days as a freshman to his final year in first-class cricket, 1866. C. G. had a style distinctly his own. Essentially a back player with a solid defence, he allowed the good ball to come on to and be deadened by a straight bat. He excelled in cutting, and when he chose to punish the bad ball in front of the wicket he was not afraid to hit in the air. A very wristy player, he responded to the suggestion that he risked being caught off his adventurous leg-side shots by saying that if he did not send the ball over long leg's head or out of the ground then he deserved to be out.

He enjoyed playing at The Oval, but disliked Lord's, being openly critical of the rough wickets there during his time. In fact, the highest score he made at Lord's was 64 for MCC against Oxford University in 1865, the year after he had come down from Cambridge. This was, according to *Wisden*, the only time in his life that he was leg before wicket.

He played for Worcestershire, was president of the Club in 1909 and 1910, and also won a blue for real tennis. He was Member of Parliament for East Worcestershire from 1868 to 1874.

As we shall see, the political connections were strong. He was a nephew of Gladstone, and one of his sisters married Talbot, the distinguished MP for Oxford University.

C. G. Lyttelton inherited the Viscountcy and Barony of Cobham in 1888 on the death of the Duke of Buckingham, and in physical stature he mirrored his impressive titles. He was a Railway Commissioner and a Trustee of the National Portrait Gallery as well as a farmer. Spy depicted him as 'Cricket, Railways and Agriculture', but, to the chagrin of his friends, he did not appear in first-class cricket after the age of 25 although he maintained his interest in the game and was president of MCC in 1886. A batting average of 27.15 in 35 first-class matches is a good record for the time.

The eldest of his four sons, John Cavendish, played three times for Worcestershire in the mid-20s without suggesting that he was really of first-class standard. He had a passion for the game, however, and was president of MCC in 1935, and Treasurer from 1938 until his death in 1949 by which time he had also been president of Worcestershire for 13 years. The Ninth Viscount Cobham worked hard in his capacity as Treasurer of MCC, giving substance to the post, and he set up investigations into the state of and possible improvements in youth cricket.

He was Conservative MP for Droitwich from 1910 to 1916, and Parliamentary Secretary of State for War for the first eight months of the Second World War.

The Tenth Viscount Cobham was also a president and Treasurer of MCC, but he was a far better cricketer than his father. He had no innate ability but observed keenly and worked hard, turning himself first into a good club and then a competent county cricketer. He led Worcestershire with infectious enthusiasm in the years immediately before the Second World War, when he was C. J. Lyttelton, and he batted with the maxim that a great bowler could be hit as far as an ordinary one. He was vice-captain to Errol Holmes on the MCC tour of Australia and New Zealand, 1935-36, and he was associated with clubs like I Zingari, Free Foresters and Butterflies. Governor General of New Zealand from 1957 to 1962, his last first-class match was for his own XI against MCC, at Auckland, in 1961, when, at the age of 51, he hit 44 in 21 minutes, including two sixes.

We have leaped ahead, and must return to the Lyttelton brotherhood of the early part of the century.

George William Spencer Lyttelton was not, perhaps, as good a cricketer as some of his brothers, but he was in the Cambridge side during his two years in residence, hitting 114 for the university against Cambridgeshire. As he averaged 20.75 in his brief career, captured 33 wickets and made 11 catches and six stumpings, he was obviously of no mean ability.

He was a gifted musician, on the Executive Committee of the Royal College of Music, and, although from a family with strong Tory loyalties, was chief private secretary to the Prime Minister, W. E. Gladstone, his uncle, from 1892 until 1894.

Arthur Temple Lyttelton played only one first-class match, for MCC in 1872, did not make the XI at Cambridge and became Bishop of Southampton. Robert Henry, too, failed to win a blue at Cambridge except for real tennis, and his first-class cricket was limited to MCC and I Zingari. He was, however, noted for his writing on the game, being a co-author, with A. G. Steel, of the *Badminton Library – Cricket* and a persuasive advocate for changes in the lbwlaw, believing at one time that if the batsman stopped the ball with any part of his body save his head, he should be out.

Edward Lyttelton took holy orders. He was a fine all round sportsman who captained Cambridge at cricket, excelled at fives and athletics, represented Middlesex for some years and played soccer for England. He became head master first of Haileybury, then of Eton (1905-16). Which brings us to the Hon Alfred Lyttelton.

In September 1884, a famous Ape cartoon in *Vanity Fair* was titled 'English Cricket'. It depicted Alfred Lyttelton crouching behind the stumps, the accompanying text describing him as 'an excellent young man of good manners and of good report'. At that time, Alfred Lyttelton was 27 years old and was already well established in the legal profession. He was second 'devil', or drudge, to the Attorney General, and a distinguished career in sport lay behind him. In government business lay ahead.

He had kept wicket for England against Australia in the first Test match to be played in England, 1880, the year after he had come down from Cambridge where he had been in the side for four years, and captain in the last. Never available to tour, he had played for England in 1882, the match when England were beaten by seven runs and brought the term 'Ashes' into being.

He was next seen in Test cricket in the last two encounters of the 1884 season, at Lord's and The Oval. The Oval match was the first occasion when all 11 players of one side bowled in a Test. McDonnell, 103; Murdoch, 211; and Scott, 102, all made centuries for Australia. As a last resort Grace put Lyttelton on to bowl while he himself kept wicket. Lyttelton's lobs took four wickets for eight runs. He finished with 4-19 in 12 overs. These were the only wickets he took in first-class cricket but his Test record as a wicketkeeper turned bowler is unlikely to be beaten.

In the words of Lord Curzon, 'No boyish hero was ever quite such a hero' as Alfred Lyttelton. He touched everything to which he turned his hand with brilliance. Tall, vigorous and graceful in movement, he was a leading athlete and a top player in racquets and fives. He gave up racquets after his third year at Cambridge in order to concentrate on tennis, and he became the leading amateur tennis player of his day.

He was a soccer player of excitement and flair, capable of running the length of the field to score. He was in the England side that lost 3-1 to Scotland in 1877 – he scored the single goal – having played in the losing Old Etonians side at the FA Cup Final against Wanderers the previous year. Kenyon-Slaney was in the same side.

As a cricketer, he was a safe and quick wicketkeeper who claimed 134 catches and 70 stumpings in his 101 first-class matches; as a batsman, he was ever bright, straight and forceful. The highest of his seven centuries was for Middlesex against Gloucestershire, at Clifton, in August 1883. He and I. D. Walker shared a second-wicket stand of 324. According to *Cricket; A Weekly Record of the Game*, this was 'the longest stand ever made by two batsmen in a first-class match', and the runs came at an astonishing rate. In his book on the Walker family, Bettesworth gives an account of the stand: 'Until after lunch, when the score was over a hundred, the two amateurs played a sound game without taking any risks, but presently they began to let themselves go, and eventually were hitting against each other, with the apparent object of seeing who could hit the greater number of balls over the ropes. Nothing in this long partnership was more noticeable than the way in which Mr Lyttelton made the 16 runs which brought his score to an hundred. When he stood at 84 he had to face Mr W. G. Grace, but instead of taking extreme precautions, as is generally done in these days when a man is nearing his hundred, he hit every ball of the over to the boundary with tremendous force. At one time during the afternoon 170 runs were put on in an hour. Such a complete mastery was obtained over the bowling that the strategy of the Gloucestershire captain was at last confined to spreading his men out in the long-field in the hope that one of them would be able to cover himself with glory by making a catch. At length, when the partnership had lasted for three hours and 19 minutes, and had produced 324 runs – a record at the time – Mr Walker was caught at mid-off for 145, an innings which included two sixes and 17 fours. Mr Lyttelton survived him only a short time.'

Cricket stated that 226 runs were scored in an hour and three-quarters and had the highest praise for Lyttelton's 181 which included a six and 21 fours. He offered two chances, but his batting 'showed all the power which has always marked his play, and his performance was the more noteworthy as he had only previously taken part in two big matches this season.'

Gloucestershire, it must be remembered, were one of the strongest counties of the period, and W. G. Grace ended the innings with a bowling analysis which read – 63 overs, 21 maidens, 154 runs, and the wicket of C. T. Studd.

Essentially, Lyttelton was one of those natural sportsmen who could come to the game after long spells of inactivity and immediately find his best form. Above all, he did everything with an engaging smile and a generosity of spirit that captivated his opponents whatever the game.

He was, too, an able and serious student, and he put his studies for the Bar before his sporting interests. When Ivo Bligh's side went to Australia in 1882-83 in an attempt to regain the Ashes, it had been hoped that Alfred Lyttelton would be one of the team, and, indeed, act as captain. But his serious legal studies were just beginning, and, regretfully, he felt he could not make the trip. It was then that Bligh, his close friend, took over.

He twice served on the MCC committee for periods, and he was president in 1898. He also played for Worcestershire, the county of the family home, but business and political activities began to take precedence, and Alfred Lyttelton, K.C., the most gifted athlete of his generation, played no more first-class cricket after 1887 when he was 30 years old. A first-class career record of 4,429 runs in 101 matches (average 27.85) with 12 centuries and 204 wicket keeping victims remains impressive indeed.

Politics began in June 1895, when he was elected Conservative MP for Warwick, and, in 1903, Balfour appointed him Secretary of State for the Colonies. He lost his post when the Liberals came to power in December 1905, but he was elected Member for St George's, Hanover Square. He was the sitting member when, in June 1913, he was taken ill. An operation was deemed necessary but he died following it.

Lyttelton was then only 56, a constant worker in philanthropic areas, a man of warmth, and deeply mourned. About the only sport which he did not master totally was golf which he took up late in life. He made enormous strides but his government duties prevented him from playing as much as was necessary. He had not quite come down to scratch before he died. Of the Lyttelton family, it was truly said: 'A greater galaxy of talent never issued from beneath an English roof-tree.'

During the period in which Alfred Lyttelton held the post of Secretary of State for the Colonies, four other men who had appeared in first-class cricket held government office, and a fifth, Lord Harris, was Governor of Bombay. Of Lord Hamilton, A. F. Jeffreys and Sir W. H. Walrond, we have already spoken. We should now turn to H. W. Forster, Junior Lord of the Treasury from 1902 to 1905, and Financial Secretary to the War Office in the Coalition Government, 1915 to 1919, when he was raised to the peerage as Baron Forster of Lepe and appointed Governor General of Australia. As he was also president of MCC in 1919, it could be said that it was his vintage year.

Born at Catford and educated at Eton, Henry Forster was a batsman in the classical mould, upright, front-foot and strong on the off side. He also bowled slow left-arm very accurately and was an outstanding fielder. He won his blue as a freshman at Oxford in 1887 and played for the Gentlemen against the Players at both The Oval and Lord's the same year.

He hit 60 not out and took three wickets in his first Varsity match. Much was expected of him, but the promise was never quite fulfilled. He was essentially a hard, fast wicket batsman, and when Oxford met Cambridge at Lord's in 1888, the ground was a muddy swamp. Forster was bowled by Sammy Woods for one, but his brief innings contained an incident which went into cricket folk lore. Francis Ford bowled him a ball which pitched halfway down the wicket. In attempting to clout the delivery, Forster hit the ball with the splice of his bat. The ball looped gently to mid-on where the fielder dropped the catch. It was generally reported that this was the worst ball, the worst stroke and the worst miss ever seen at Lord's!

No sooner had he come down from Oxford than Forster entered upon his public career, when he was elected as Conservative Member for Sevenoaks in Kent in 1892. He held the seat until he became Governor General of Australia 27 years later.

His parliamentary work left him little time for cricket, but he played for Hampshire as much as was possible and led the county in 1890, succeeding F. E. Lacey as captain. Sir Francis was to be secretary of

MCC at the time when Forster was president. Forster played for Hampshire until 1895 by which time the county had attained first-class status so that he is one of the few men who was actually appearing in first-class cricket when a sitting Member of Parliament.

His batting always looked fine without producing the anticipated results, but in a career which lasted ten years and covered 43 first-class games, he took 135 wickets at 21.65. When he gave up cricket he turned his attention to golf. He studied the game with the same thoroughness that he brought to all else that he did, and he was soon among the best amateur golfers in the country. He was also a very keen yachtsman, a long-time member of the Royal Yacht Squadron.

Handsome, well-built, with a great deal of tact, charm and courtesy, he was highly respected as Governor of Australia where his sporting record and interests enhanced his popularity.

He had been made a Privy Councillor in 1917 and was an honorary Doctor of Civil Law and an honorary Fellow of New College, Oxford. He spent five years in Australia during which he unveiled a plaque to the great all-rounder Giffen during the Test series of 1924-25. A one-time president of Kent, he died early in 1936 at the age of 69.

The majority of cricketers were unable to combine the responsibilities of their parliamentary work with pursuing the game at a high level although Percy Thornton reconciled the post of secretary of Middlesex from 1870 to 1898 with being MP for Clapham from 1892 to 1910. He was the cousin of the famous hitter C. I. Thornton but a lesser player than his relation. He played for Cambridge in 1864 without winning his blue and his one game for the county, of which he was honorary secretary, was in 1872 when he scored 3 and 0 against Surrey at Prince's in the last fixture of the season. He played then only because Middlesex were very short of regular members of the side.

In 1902, Percy Cross Standing was lamenting in his two-volume *Cricket of To-day and Yesterday*: 'Alas that the cricket of politics does not run in double harness with the politics of cricket! Parliament has taken too many of our finest bats and bowlers, and has not given one of them back to us.'

He then lists an entire XI, headed naturally enough by Alfred Lyttelton, who had been lost to the House of Commons. At number three, one place above Forster, Standing has George Kemp, later to be Sir George Kemp, and, after 1913, Baron Rochdale.

Born in Rochdale, Kemp was educated first at Mill Hill School and then at Shrewsbury, going up to Cambridge in the autumn of 1884. He hit a century in the Freshmen's Match the following summer and won his blue the same year. The captain of the Cambridge side was the man destined to be Lord Hawke, and Kemp played a significant part in the victory over Oxford.

Kemp had arrived at Trinity College with a fine reputation as a sportsman, and he was to be one of the five outstanding cricketers at the university during the 1880s. He represented Cambridge in the doubles at lawn tennis, and won the mile at Trinity in 1886. At cricket he was particularly strong on the off side, stylish and purposeful in all he did.

Kemp played for Lancashire during his first year at Cambridge. He began with 0 against MCC, but, in his second match, he hit 109 in three hours against Yorkshire, with 17 fours. Lancashire were beaten by eight wickets, but Kemp had become the first Lancastrian to score a century in the Roses Match. He was six weeks beyond his 19th birthday, and greatness was predicted.

In 1886, Cambridge enjoyed a good season, and George Kemp topped the batting averages, but, surprisingly, they were beaten in the Varsity match. Handsome, with wavy hair and a slight moustache, Kemp was attracting more and more attention. With two wins in succession behind them, Cambridge entertained Yorkshire, and, having been bowled out for 74, they began their second innings 80 runs in arrears, but they went on to win the match by 26 runs, 'a result due entirely to the exceptionally fine cricket of one batsman, Mr Kemp.'

Cricket: A Weekly Record of the Game continued: 'For three hours and a half he was batting in the most brilliant form, and with the exception of one hit which nearly came to hand when he had got 87, his play was without a fault. He went in first wicket down with the total at 10 and was seventh out, having contributed 125 out of 213 while in.' The quality of Kemp's innings can be judged from a Yorkshire attack which consisted of bowlers of the calibre of Peate, Emmett, Ulyett, Bates and Peel.

Success seemed unabated when, chosen for the Gentlemen of England against the Australians, Kemp hit 83 out of 149 scored while he was at the wicket. He and Roller of Surrey put on 93 for the sixth wicket.

Two days after this game at The Oval, he hit 103 for Cambridge University against Yorkshire at Bramall Lane. The innings occupied just 160 minutes, and once again he won lavish praise. Cricket could write with justification 'that he is to be regarded as the most promising of the younger order of amateur batsmen.'

The brightness of 1886 quickly began to fade, however, not through any dreadful loss of form, but because Kemp was able to give little time to cricket. He played scarcely at all in 1887 and did not appear in the Varsity match. Although he reappeared the following year and scored 66 and 56 against the Australians, and played in the Varsity match, he did not make himself available for Lancashire. Indeed, his career for the county and in first-class cricket was almost at an end. He played a little until 1892, but in seven years he appeared only 18 times for Lancashire. Politics was already taking over.

In 1895, he was elected Liberal MP for the Heywood Division of Lancashire. He was only 29 years old, and although his last first-class match was for A. J. Webbe's XI in 1899, he was virtually lost to the game, as a player at least. He was listed as one of the parliamentarians who had been invited to tour the British Empire, playing cricket in Canada, Australia and Ceylon, in 1897. The tour was to have lasted some 90 days, but there is no evidence it ever took place. Such stuff as dreams are made of.

He had a rapid rise in politics becoming Parliamentary Private Secretary to the Financial Secretary to the Admiralty, but then went to fight in the Boer War. He served with the Imperial Yeomanry and was Mentioned in Dispatches.

Kemp, knighted in 1903, maintained his interest in cricket as Vice president of Lancashire, and his career in politics when he won two elections in 1910 to serve as Member for the North West Division of Manchester. Created Baron Rochdale in 1913, he commanded a Battalion of the Lancashire Fusiliers in the First World War. He never lost his allegiance to the army, being a territorial officer for over 30 years. From 1929, he was Lord Lieutenant of Middlesex, and his interest in outdoor pursuits never left him. He was a keen shot until the last years of his life which ended in 1945 at the age of 78.

Well may Percy Standing have rued the loss to Parliament of so fine a cricketer, for who else in their first-class career could boast that their three centuries had all been scored off the bowling of one of the great Yorkshire sides.

Standing also mourned the loss to cricket of Sir Arthur Priestley, but, as Priestley's career average was 7.32 from 18 matches, and he did not bowl, it is harder to share his feelings. Priestley was MP for Grantham from 1900 until 1918, but this did not prevent him from going on tour of North America with Bosanquet's side in 1901. Priestley was an avid tourist; this was the fourth trip he had made in seven years.

He had been a member of R. S. Lucas' party who, early in 1895, were the first group of English cricketers to tour the West Indies. He appeared in the eight first-class matches on this tour and, opening the innings in British Guiana – he usually batted well down the order – he made 36, the highest score of the match and the highest of his career.

No doubt heightened by this success, he took his own side to the West Indies a year later. Unfortunately, Lord Hawke also took a side to the West Indies at the same time, for there had been some misunderstanding as to whether or not his Lordship had accepted invitations from the local authorities. Priestley's team had been invited by Barbados and Jamaica, and although Hawke and Priestley met they were unable to come to an amicable settlement. Both tours went ahead. The later publication of correspondence between the two men revealed that Hawke was rather arbitrary in his treatment of Priestley.

This time Priestley, who captained the side, played in nine first-class matches, batted mostly at number ten or nine, and kept wicket in one game. His batting average for the nine matches (15 innings) was 2.64, and he did not reach double figures.

His enthusiasm was unquenchable, and he was off to the United States and Canada with Ranjitsinhji's team in 1899. This side contained some fine cricketers, for, apart from Ranji himself, there were Jessop, Woods, C. L. Townsend, Stoddart, MacLaren and Bosanquet. Priestley did not play in a first-class match on the tour, and the same was true in 1901 when Bosanquet's party was also a strong one.

In fact, Arthur Priestley made only one first-class appearance outside the West Indies, when, in 1895, he played for MCC against Warwickshire. MCC won by an innings, and Priestley, at number nine, scored but two.

On his death in 1993, Priestley was described by *Wisden* as an MCC member who was 'not particularly prominent in the game itself'. One cannot argue with such an epitaph, but here was a man with a passion for cricket who, by his willingness to journey far, earned himself a place in the statistics of the game as having appeared in 18 first-class matches. This is considerably more than Pearce, Wentworth, Ward, Sanderson and McNeill who managed just ten between them.

Sir William Pearce – he was knighted in 1915 – was a right-handed batsman and bowler who was educated at Malvern and played three matches for Kent under Lord Harris in June 1878. The games, against Nottinghamshire, Hampshire and Derbyshire, were all away and were condensed into a period of 16 days.

In the last of the three, at the Racecourse, Derby, he caught and bowled Curgenven and bowled Smith and Mycroft with successive deliveries in Derbyshire's first innings to perform the hat-trick. He hit 6 and 14, his highest first-class score; Kent won by 82 runs; and Pearce, who was 25 years old at the time, was never seen in first-class cricket again. He did play for Essex before the county was first-class, but his life was devoted mostly to business and politics.

Pearce, who had been born in Poplar and was to die in Walmer where he made his home, studied at the Royal College of Chemistry and the School of Mines. He was a director of the chemical manufacturers Spencer, Chapman and Messel Ltd, and he was vice-president of the Federation of British Industries. He served on the London County Council, was Justice of the Peace for the County of London, and, from 1906 until 1922, he was Liberal MP for Limehouse.

He retired from the House at the age of 69, died in 1932, and left behind the mystery as to why so little was seen of him in the first-class game and conjecture as to what he might have achieved had he played more.

The same might be said of Captain Bruce Canning Vernon-Wentworth, as he later became known, for in three matches for MCC between 1897 and 1900 he batted with consistency and averages 26 from five innings. Educated at Harrow and at Sandhurst, Wentworth served in the Grenadier Guards and lived at Wentworth Castle, near Barnsley. He had a zest for politics; three times he contested Barnsley on behalf of the Conservative Party and three times his home town rejected him. Eventually, in 1893, he found the safer haven of Brighton where he remained as Conservative MP until 1906.

This means that Wentworth was one of the few men whose first-class cricket career, brief as it was, was played while he was a Member of Parliament. Like George Kemp, he was invited to join the parliamentary cricket team to tour the British Empire in 1898 – the tour that did not take place.

In Wentworth's case, appearances in first-class cricket were, no doubt, reduced by his military and political duties; the appearances of Arnold Sandwith Ward were restricted by his multi-talents and interests. Ward had an exceptional pedigree. He was the great-grandson of Thomas Arnold of Rugby, and his mother was the novelist Mrs Humphry Ward, who embodied in her novels the belief that Christianity could be revitalised by emphasising its social mission. She gave much of her life to social and philanthropic works and to actively opposing the extension of the franchise to women.

Arnold Ward inherited his mother's vitality and intelligence. He went to both Eton, where he was in the XI and Uppingham, before going up to Balliol where he captained the cricket team. He played for Hertfordshire from 1896 to 1899, and for Buckinghamshire for the first five years of this century. His one first-class match was for Oxford in 1899 when he scored 6 and 2, and took 0-52 with his right-arm medium-pace bowling. It is difficult to comprehend how he had any time to spare for cricket.

A brilliant scholar, he won the Chancellor's Latin Verse Prize at Oxford in 1897, and the Craven Scholarship the following year. He was special correspondent for *The Times* in Egypt, Sudan and India between 1899 and 1902 and was called to the Bar in 1903. He contested the Cricklade Division of Wiltshire without success in 1906, but was elected Unionist MP for West Hertfordshire 1910-18. He was also a lieutenant in the Hertfordshire Yeomanry and served in Egypt in 1914 and 1915 and later saw service in Cyprus. But to the end, he insisted his one recreation was cricket.

For Lancelot Sanderson, perhaps, it might have been more than a recreation had he been more favoured by fortune and less engulfed by work. He was a long standing member of MCC, served on the committee for some years and was an auditor of the club at the time of his death in 1944. A Lancastrian by birth, he was educated at Elstree and Harrow, and, in 1882, had match figures of 7-66 against Eton at Lord's. He was tall, well built, bowled slow right-arm, fielded effectively and was a most sound and capable batsman.

Sanderson went up to Trinity College, Cambridge, full of high hopes. He played in the Freshmen's Match and scored 37 not out for Hawke's side, and yet he was not to appear in a first-class match for Cambridge.

In 1884, he played for Lancashire in their last match of the season, against Somerset. Lancashire won by ten wickets, but Sanderson was out for 0 and never played for the county again. There was some consolation in a rackets blue in his last year at university, but, for the most part, he was lost to cricket.

He was called to the Bar in 1886, and two years later, he appeared in his second, and last, first-class match. It was for MCC against Cambridge University, at Cambridge. When he went to the wicket MCC were 35-5, but he and Eaton added 105 of which Sanderson made 61. The Cambridge attack was formidable and included Sammy Woods, F. G. J. Ford and C. D. Buxton. Sanderson made 10 in the second innings, MCC won a fine game by 17 runs, and from that point it was law and politics for Sanderson. From 1901 to 1915, he was Recorder for Wigan, and he took silk in 1903. Two years later he unsuccessfully contested the City of Carlisle as a Unionist candidate.

In 1910, however, he was elected MP for the Appleby Division of Westmorland. He stood down in 1915, was knighted and went to India as Chief Justice of Bengal. In 1918, he was also Vice-Chancellor of Calcutta University. He returned to England in 1926, became a Privy Councillor and spent his remaining days watching the game which, perhaps, had not served him quite as well as it might have done. In spite of that bowling success against Eton, he did not send down a ball in his two first-class matches.

Ronald John McNeill has no cause for complaint. When he died in 1934 *Wisden* ignored his long and often passionate political career and stated simply in one line that he was 'in the Harrow XI of 1880'. What *Wisden* does not mention is that McNeill batted number ten for MCC against Oxford University, at Oxford, in May 1885, and was run out for two. On the strength of this one match and this one innings, a politician of some controversy claims first-class status.

Ronald McNeill was the only surviving son of a Scottish landowner who had settled in Ireland. From Harrow, he went to Christ Church, Oxford, where he took a second class in Modern History, 1884. There is no record of his cricketing achievements, save his one game for MCC, and he followed the well-trodden path into law, being called to the Bar in 1888.

In the legal profession he established a record, for, at 6ft 6ins, he was the tallest barrister of his time. Impulsive, but generous, he lost interest in the law and turned to journalism. He became assistant editor of *St*

James's Gazette in 1899 and editor a year later. This interested him until 1904 when he decided upon a political career.

His tenacity can be evidenced from the fact that he unsuccessfully fought four elections; at West Aberdeenshire in 1906; at South Aberdeen City in February 1907, and in January 1910; and at Kircudbrightshire in December 1910. In compensation for these endeavours, he was Conservative candidate for the by-election for the St Augustine's Division of Kent in 1911, and he was unopposed. He held the seat, later renamed the Canterbury Division of Kent, for 16 years.

McNeill remained active in other fields. He was assistant editor to the 11th edition of the *Encyclopaedia Britannica*, 1906-11, and contributed a variety of articles to a variety of publications on topics as diverse as sewers and the history of Australia and New Zealand. In politics he was a die-hard, and in the matter of tariff reform a wholehogger.

There was passion and impetuosity in his politics, and during the debate on Home Rule, November 1912, he threw a blue book at the First Lord of the Admiralty, Winston Churchill. He always held extreme opinions on controversial matters, and it came as something of a surprise when Bonar Law appointed him Parliamentary Under Secretary for Foreign Affairs in 1922.

Bonar Law's judgement proved to be inspired. McNeill became noted for his skill, industry and patience, and he won the high regard of all, including the sceptics. In 1924, he was made a Privy Councillor, and the following year was appointed Financial Secretary to the Treasury, under, ironically enough, Winston Churchill.

In the autumn of 1927, he became Chancellor of the Duchy of Lancaster, given a seat in the cabinet and raised to the peerage. He took the title of Baron Cushendun, the village in Antrim where he held his estates. As British Representative to the League of Nations, he made a great impact with his arguments against disarmament, and, in the closing months of 1928, when Austen Chamberlain was ill, acted as Secretary of State for Foreign Affairs.

He died in Ireland in 1934 at the age of 73. The fire and the passion were with him to the end; the cricket, it seems, had long since been forgotten.

If Baron Cushendun, perhaps, forgot cricket, cricket, it appears, forgot R. E. Prothero, First Lord Ernle. His obituary in the 7th Edition of *Wisden Cricketers' Almanack* (1938) occupies less than two lines:

PROTHERO, ROWLAND EDMUND, LORD ERNLE, PC, MVO, who died at Wantage on July 1, aged 85, was in the Marlborough XI 1870 and 1871.

Scant recognition of a man who was a cabinet minister, a president of MCC, and the scorer of a century in first-class cricket!

The son of a clergyman who played cricket at Oxford in 1839, Rowland Prothero was educated at Marlborough, and he was in the XI in 1870 and 1871, but what *Wisden* fails to mention is that he did bowl well against Cheltenham and that when he played against Rugby at Lord's in 1871 he hit 24 which included five runs for hitting the ball into a bush. The following season, he made his first-class debut. He appeared for the Gentlemen of England against Oxford University on the Magdalen College Ground at Cowley. He batted number 11 in the first innings and was unbeaten on 11, then he opened in the second innings when the Gentlemen needed 16 to win; he was unbeaten on eight. That the Gentlemen of England won so easily was due in no small measure to Prothero who, with Buchanan, bowled unchanged in the first Oxford innings and took 5-34. In the second innings, he took 3-44.

Nothing is then heard of Prothero in first-class cricket until 1875 when he played the first of his four games for Hampshire spread over a period of eight years. This was the year in which he graduated from Balliol College. He became a Fellow of All Saints and was called to the Bar in 1878. Perhaps in celebration of becoming a barrister, Prothero made his second appearance for the Gentlemen of England in 1879. The opponents were again Oxford University, captained by A. H. Heath whose career in cricket and politics we have already detailed. Prothero's right-arm medium pace bowling seems, by this time, to have become a little rusty, for he sent down just five overs in the second innings and took 0-7.

He batted number 11 in the first innings and was four not out in a total of 74. The university made 47, and Prothero was promoted in the second Gentlemen's innings. He and Fryer, coming together at 84-5, shared a century stand. Prothero made 110 in a match in which nobody else on his side reached 50. He was some three months short of his 28th birthday.

The first-class cricket field saw him for the last time in August 1883, when he played for Hampshire against Somerset, scoring 7 and 19, and taking 1-30 and 0-6. In six first-class matches, he averaged 31.66 from ten innings, took 10-181 and held seven catches. It is not a record to be ignored, particularly as he had scored one of only ten centuries made in the England season of 1879. W. G. Grace scored two of them.

Prothero became JP for the County of London, and from 1893 until 1899, he was editor of *The Quarterly Review*. The publication had been started in 1809 as a Tory rival of the *Edinburgh Review*, but always run on impartial and liberal lines. Unquestionably, Prothero was a Tory. In 1899, he became agent to the Duke of Bedford, and two years later he was made a Member of the Royal Victorian Order. His political career was truly launched, and he was elected Conservative Member for Oxford University in 1904.

When the Coalition Government was formed in 1915 Asquith appointed Prothero president of the Board of Agriculture and Fisheries, and he remained in the post under Lloyd George until 1919, serving as a member of the cabinet. Stepping down at the age of 68, he was raised to the peerage as the First Lord Ernle.

He continued to work and to serve. He was a member of the Chamber of Commerce of London University in 1924, and the same year president of MCC. He was honoured for his contributions to agriculture, and for his concern for literature and the arts he was recognised by universities as far apart as Wales and Athens. But when he died in 1937 *Wisden* gave him those two lines, and *The Cricketer* failed even to mention his passing.

Relative Values
and Great
All-Rounders

NOT only was Sir Maurice Bonham-Carter a member of a great Liberal political family, he was also related to a long line of cricketers. His grandfather, G.W. Norman, had played for Kent in the days before first-class cricket was chronicled, and two of his uncles, Charles and Frederick Norman, won blues at Cambridge and played occasionally for Kent. A third uncle, Philip, appeared once for the Gentlemen of Kent in 1865 without distinguishing himself, but he later contributed two books to the literature of the game, *The Eton Ramblers CC, 1962-1880* and *Scores and Annals of the West Kent CC.*

Sir Maurice also had a nephew, Philip Herman Bonham-Carter, who played three first-class games for the Royal Navy between 1919 and 1929, and, through the Normans (his mother's family) he was connected with the Nepean, Jenner, Dyke, Wathen and Barnard families all of whom had first-class cricketers in their midst.

Sir Maurice's own career was somewhat limited. A middle-order right-handed batsman, a slow bowler and an occasional wicketkeeper, he was in the Winchester XI of 1898 and 1899, and the following year he went up to Balliol College, Oxford. He played in the Freshmen's Match of 1900 and hit 96, yet he did not appear in the university side until the following year. It makes one ponder the purpose of trial matches.

In 1902, he scored 86 against H. D. G. Levenson-Gower's XI and was selected for the Varsity match. Batting at number eight, he twice had the misfortune to be bowled by Dowson, the outstanding player of the match, for 0. There was consolation in that Bonham-Carter took 2-2 in Cambridge's first innings and 1-61 in the second, but that was his 13th and last game for Oxford. Some weeks later, he played for Kent at Lord's, made 16 and 1 and took 0-9. That marked the end of his first-class career.

He married Violet Asquith, daughter of the Liberal leader Herbert, who was Prime Minister from 1908 until 1916. Sir Maurice served as Asquith's Private Secretary for the last six years of the premiership, thus allowing us loosely to include him in these pages. His elder son, Mark, Baron Yarnbury, has maintained the family tradition in that he has served as a Liberal MP and is a member of MCC. Sir Maurice's granddaughter Helena is a noted actress.

Henry Fitzherbert Wright cannot claim as many cricketing relations as Maurice Bonham-Carter, although his brother-in-law, Godfrey Foljambe, played first-class cricket for MCC, and his son-in-law, James Leaf, appeared once for the Army in 1937. He was, however, 'one of several amateurs who flitted in and out of Derbyshire cricket' in the last years of the 19th and early years of the 20th century.

Wright was in the Eton XI in 1889 and went up to Trinity College, Cambridge, the following year. He played in the Freshmen's Match in 1890 and the Seniors' Match the following year, but he never played a game for Cambridge. He appeared in two matches for Derbyshire during his second year at Cambridge, against MCC and Ground and Surrey but found the opposition too strong for him. Derbyshire were not, at that time, a first-class county, and Wright's first-class career was restricted to nine matches for them in 1904 and 1905. He acquitted himself quite well, averaging 22.95 and taking four catches.

He was by then embarked on a legal career, having been called to the Bar in 1895. His links with the county of his birth were always strong, for he became both Justice of the Peace and High Sheriff, as well as Vice-chairman of the County Cricket Club.

A captain in the First Derbyshire (Howitzer) Battery of the Royal Fleet Auxiliary between 1908 and 1911, he was elected Unionist MP for the Leominster Division of Hereford in 1912. He held the seat until 1918 although he was on active service from 1914 until 1917.

Wright, along with his brother-in-law Foljambe, was a member of Lord Hawke's party that made a successful tour of India and Ceylon in the winter of 1892-93, and he also appeared in four other first-class games as well as his nine for Derbyshire. It was then he would have met Sir Samuel Hill (the surname became Hill-Wood in 1910) a more powerful sporting figure by far who played each of his 34 first-class matches for Derbyshire, 1894-1902.

Samuel Hill-Wood captained Derbyshire from 1899 to 1901 although it was only in his second year as skipper that he was able to play with any regularity. His contribution to Derbyshire cricket was immense, not least because four of his sons made a total of 83 appearances for the county between them.

Sir Samuel was one of the most prominent figures in sport in the first half of the century. He invested a great deal of money into his home town football club, Glossop, who won promotion to the First Division of the Football League in 1899, only to be relegated after one season. More significantly he then became chairman of Arsenal FC in 1927 holding the post until his death in 1949. A Hill-Wood has remained chairman of Arsenal throughout the club's great triumphs.

An Etonian, Sir Samuel Hill-Wood was fascinated by all sports and won the Waterloo Cup in 1910 and 1913 when he was a Member of Parliament. In fact he represented High Peak in Derbyshire as a Conservative for 19 years after election in 1910. In cricket, he used h⸱ money, his vision and his influence in Glossop to do much f⸜

Derbyshire CCC. He helped bring Sam Cadman to the county, and he saw that first-class cricketers turned out for his Glossop team in the Central Lancashire League. One of these was Charles Ollivierre, the first West Indian to play county cricket. Ollivierre had attracted attention when touring with the first West Indian side to come to England, in 1900. Hill-Wood saw that he played for Glossop while he was qualifying for Derbyshire through residence, and he also guaranteed the financial success of cricket in the town.

In truth, Samuel Hill-Wood was a moderate cricketer as a career average of 16.29 and 505 runs in 35 innings would suggest, but he also took 45 wickets and his commitment to the game was total. His sons followed him to Eton and into the Derbyshire side, and Wilfred, in particular, was an excellent batsman. Had he not had to dedicate so much of his life to business, he might well have played for England, but his first-class cricket as good as ended when he came down from Cambridge in 1922 although his last match for Derbyshire was not until 1936.

Samuel Hill-Wood assisted Suffolk between 1908 and 1911, but this, and his long-standing association with Arsenal Football Club, did nothing to weaken the bond with his home county.

William Bridgeman's passion for cricket was certainly every bit as great as Samuel Hill-Wood's, and he was even more of a passionate Etonian than the Derbyshire man.

The only son of a clergyman with aristocratic connections, Bridgeman was captain of the Oppidans at Eton, and it was a source of the greatest pride and pleasure to him that his three sons succeeded him as a captain. He was a life-long Etonian and was elected a Fellow of the College.

He won a scholarship to Trinity College, Cambridge, and took an upper second in classics. In his first game for the university, against C. O. Thornton's XI at the beginning of the 1887 season, he hit 44. A modest start but a month later, he gave a remarkable display at Hove. Sussex made 451, and Cambridge were 147-6 when Bridgeman, who had gone in at number seven, was joined by Martineau. The pair added 193 in 160 minutes. Bridgeman finished unbeaten on 162, a chanceless innings which included 16 fours and occupied about six hours. He and Orford put on 93 for the ninth wicket.

Bridgeman won his blue that year, but he did little in the Varsity match. The following season he appeared in the first three matches, batted low in the order and failed to reach double figures. He had virtually disappeared from important cricket although he did re-emerge for MCC against his old university in May 1894, only to be dismissed for 0. It was his final first-class innings, leaving a record of 13 matches and an average, helped by that 161 not out, of 21.23.

He had by now developed into what was described as 'a considerable gentleman cricketer', playing for Shropshire, Staffordshire, I Zingari and MCC He had also established himself as a country gentleman in Shropshire. Aidan Crawley related in later life how, at the age of eight, he was number 11 in the Crawley XI which played the Bridgeman XI at Weston Park, Shropshire, in 1916.

W. C. Bridgeman's passion was cricket, but his principal interest was politics. He maintained the family's Conservative attachment, and, from 1889 to 1892, he was Assistant Private Secretary to Viscount Knutsford. He later occupied the same post to Sir Michael Hicks Beach. In 1906, he was elected Member of Parliament for the Northern (Oswestry) Division of Shropshire, holding the seat for 23 years.

Bridgeman adhered to the Disraeli tradition of social reform, unionism and closer imperial unity. He became Junior Opposition Whip in 1911, and made such an impression in the job that Asquith appointed him Government Whip in the Coalition Government of 1916 when he was also Assistant Director of the World Trade Department.

Lloyd George then gave him even greater responsibility, making him first Parliamentary Secretary to the newly-formed Ministry of Labour, and successively, to the Board of Trade and to the Mines Department. In spite of these appointments, Bridgeman always had the greatest distrust of Lloyd George and was close friend and fervent supporter of Stanley Baldwin. It was Bridgeman's feelings towards these two men that made him one of the leaders of the Conservative revolt which brought down the Coalition Government.

Lloyd George was too restless a figure for the tranquillity that the people soon demanded. Some Conservatives, notably Churchill, believed that they should stay united with the Liberals against the common enemy, Socialism, but the majority, led by Baldwin and his friend Bridgeman, advocated the Conservatives should fight the next election as an independent party with its own programme. So large was the majority that Lloyd George was forced to resign at once. In the election which followed, the Conservatives won 344 seats, Labour rose to 142, and the Liberals were divided between supporters of Asquith, 60, and those loyal to Lloyd George, 57.

Bonar Law took office in October 1922, when Bridgeman was appointed Home Secretary. He was forced to resign through ill-health in May 1923, and Baldwin, Bridgeman's great friend and ally, succeeded him.

Baldwin's first ministry was short-lived, but so was the Labour Government which followed, and when the Conservatives were returned to power in November 1924, Bridgeman was appointed First Lord of the Admiralty. Ironically, he had succeeded another cricketer in this post, the Labour peer, Lord Chelmsford.

Bridgeman kept his position as First Lord of the Admiralty until his retirement in 1929. He fought some fierce battles in the five years in which he was in office, opposing the attempts of the Chancellor of the Exchequer, Winston Churchill, to cut expenditure on the Navy, and resuming the construction of the base at Singapore.

Perhaps Bridgeman echoed the qualities which some saw in Baldwin – common sense, honesty, plain speaking, tenacity and fair mindedness. He was certainly held in regard and affection by the Labour opposition and the miners, which cannot be said of all politicians.

When he retired in 1929 he was created Viscount Bridgeman, but, a gentle man of sympathy, humour and understanding, he had too much energy to depart entirely. In 1932, he chaired a committee of inquiry into the Post Office, and also became chairman of the BBC. He was on the governing bodies of Eton and Shrewsbury, and he was a strong church man, ably supported by his wife Caroline, a forceful woman who succeeded him as a BBC governor and who was always politically active.

But above all, cricket was his passion. He was an assiduous committee member and an avid spectator, watching cricket at Lord's to within a few weeks of his death in August 1934. He was president of MCC in 1931, and, in February 1933, he was one of the deputation of four who went from MCC to the Dominions Office in an attempt to calm the storm that had arisen over body-line. Another member of that deputation was Sir Stanley Jackson who served with Bridgeman for a short time in the Conservative Government of 1922-23.

Like Bridgeman, Jackson was indeed something of a cricketer. He won all the honours the world of cricket has to give: president of MCC in 1921; a Trustee of the Club; captain of England, Harrow and Cambridge; chairman of Test Selectors; and, on the death of Lord Hawke, president of Yorkshire. His nephews, J. M. and T. A. L. Brocklebank, appeared in first-class cricket as did his brother-in-law, Major J. P. Wilson, who followed him to Harrow, Cambridge and into the Yorkshire XI. The gods gave 'Jacker' everything, nor did they ever take their gifts away.

A. G. Moyes wrote of Jackson: 'He had that touch of genius that can vary the orthodox with the unorthodox and he batted in the same way in mud as on a dry turf.' Jackson also bowled a brisk medium pace off a shortish run and was able to spin the ball into the batsman with a natural flick of the wrist. In an age of splendour for cricket, he was a jewel in the crown. What is so remarkable is that his magnificent record as an all-rounder was achieved without a tour to Australia, for business always came first for him. Cricket was a pastime, and his one tour was with Hawke's side to India in 1892-93 when he was still at university.

From the outset Jacker's talent was recognised. Son of Lord Allerton, he was at preparatory school where the headmaster prophesied, 'That lad will one day be captain of England.' His exceptional sporting prowess allowed him to move into Harrow more smoothly than most, and he prospered throughout his days on the hill although he did not give too much concern to his academic studies. Jackson was joined at Harrow by another future England captain, Archie MacLaren, and a future Prime Minister, Winston Churchill, was fag to them both.

The match against Eton at Lord's in 1888 proved to be something of a turning point in Jackson's career. He scored 21 and 59, and Harrow, having been bowled out for 80 and trailing by 26 on the first innings, won a famous victory by 156 runs. Jackson took 6-40 and 5-28, a performance which inspired the Harrow song *A Gentleman's A-Bowling*.

Jackson led the side the following year, enjoyed a fine all-round season and ended in triumph with an innings of 68 and five wickets in a nine-wicket victory over Eton. All was now set for his arrival at Trinity College, Cambridge where he was dubbed Lord Harrow. He was not to be preoccupied with academic studies and graduated with an ordinary BA. His honours were on the cricket field.

His first-class debut came against C. I. Thornton's XI at Cambridge. He scored 17 and 19 not out, and he played a significant part in his side's four-wicket victory. A week later, he captured four wickets, and, at the end of May, took 12-114 as the university beat Yorkshire by nine wickets. He won his blue, Oxford were well beaten, and he made his debut for Yorkshire in the Roses match.

He was to win his blue in all four seasons at Cambridge, and he had the unusual distinction of captaining the XI in both 1892 and 1893 when Cambridge won by 266 runs. Shortly after his last Varsity match, Jackson made his Test debut. He hit 91 and 5 against Australia at Lord's and followed this with 103, run out, in the victory at The Oval. He declined to play in the third Test as Yorkshire had a vital match at Sussex in which victory brought them the County Championship.

'Jacker' was now accepted as one of the great all-round cricketers in the world, but business was to prevent him from ever giving his full attention to the game. Perhaps one of the reasons for his greatness was that cricket was never more than a game to him. He still managed to hit 1,000 runs in a season ten times and to do the 'double' in 1898.

The Jackson family fortune was derived from W. L. Jackson and Sons

Ltd, as it became, a tannery and currying works in Leeds. When Stanley Jackson's father, William Lawies Jackson, inherited it, it was close to bankruptcy. W. L. Jackson first resurrected and modernised the firm, and then made it very prosperous. He had political aspirations, served 11 years on Leeds Council and took the Tory group to a position of control. Having been defeated in one election, he fought another to become MP for Leeds in 1880. With the friendship and patronage of Lord Randolph Churchill, he became first Financial Secretary to the Treasury in Salisbury's Government, and then Chief Secretary for Ireland in Balfour's ministry. He was sworn a Privy Councillor in 1889, but his career in Parliament ended in 1892. This did not quench the future Lord Allerton's thirst for work, and he was engaged in numerous projects and chairman of several committees. He became the first Conservative Mayor of Leeds.

His father's political connections were to be of little help to Jackson when he turned his attention to the Conservative party. He was to find no Lord Randolph Churchill to act as his patron.

In the early part of the century, Jackson worked hard in the family firm. His commitments prevented him from playing more than nine games in 1903, and he appeared in just four matches in his last two seasons, 1906 and 1907.

His record in the closing years of the 19th century had, however, placed him among the forefront of cricketers. Many felt he should have succeeded Grace as England's captain in 1899, for he was the senior amateur in the side, but MacLaren, who had led England in Australia, was appointed. In the words of *Vanity Fair*, 'Most people were grieved (and some aggrieved) when, on W. G. Grace's retirement from big matches, he was not called upon to captain the English XI.' If Jackson himself was angered, he took it out on the Australians for, although his bowling was badly used by MacLaren, he batted splendidly and hit 118 in the final Test, at The Oval. He and Hayward shared an opening partnership of 185 which, at the time, was the best opening stand by either side in the 56 Tests they had then played against each other and the highest English partnership for any wicket in a Test in England.

Jackson hit 1847 runs that season, average 45.04, with five centuries. He was to play in only one first-class match during the next two years.

In October 1899, the Boer Republics in South Africa rebelled. The British Army was sent out to crush the uprising. They were ill-prepared for the war that they were to fight, and this is a period of military history that is not remembered with an emphasis on glory. By the time Jackson was commissioned as a Captain in the Third (Militia) Battalion of the King's Own (Royal Lancaster) Regiment in January 1900, Ladysmith and Mafeking were under siege.

Milligan, one of Jackson's Yorkshire team-mates, was killed in an attempt to relieve Mafeking, and another Yorkshireman, Frank Mitchell, so loved the country in which he fought that he returned there after the war and became the Springbok captain.

More British soldiers were to die of illnesses like typhus and cholera than were to be killed by the Boers. Jackson himself was struck down by enteric fever in the summer of 1900 and was invalided home to England. He recovered well on the sea journey, but he was still weak and convalescing when he agreed to play for the Gentlemen against the Players at Scarborough. Against an attack that included Hirst and Rhodes, he hit 134 and 42. He had not held a bat for a year, and it was to be more than a year before he held one again.

He returned to the Boer War early in 1901. He found himself responsible for guarding lines of communication and was eventually Commanding Officer at Landsberg. His mother died while he was on active service, and he returned to England in January 1902, a man changed and affected by recent experiences.

He had played only one first-class innings in two years, but he returned to cricket as if he had never been away. He played in all five Tests against Australia, hit 128 at Old Trafford, scored more runs than any other England batsman and topped the averages. He had returned to the game with a century in under two and a half hours for Yorkshire against Essex at Leyton. Even more sensationally, immediately after the first Test, he took 4-30 and 5-12 as Yorkshire beat the Australians on a rain-affected wicket at Headingley. The Australians were bowled out for 23 in their second innings, with Hirst (5-9) and Jackson bowling unchanged.

In August, on the eve of his wedding to Julia Harrison-Broadley, eldest daughter of the Conservative MP for Brough in the East Riding, Jackson was featured as A Flannelled Fighter in Spy's series of cartoons for *Vanity Fair*, 'Men of the Day'. He was described as having 'a jaunty step, a lordly manner, and exceeding confidence in himself', and it must be agreed that the opinions of those who met him, suggest that he was always something of a patrician.

He still had commitments as a soldier, to the *Yorkshire Post* as a director and, above all, to the family business. He was able to play little in 1903, and, on four occasions during his cricketing life he refused invitations to tour Australia because of business calls, but 1905 was to be his annus mirabillis.

At last MacLaren was passed over in favour of Jackson who led England in all five Tests against Australia. He was to win the toss in each and England were to win the series handsomely. Having bowled out England for 196 in the first Test, Australia, at 129-1, looked set for a massive lead, but Jackson dismissed Noble, Hill and Darling, the Australian captain born on the same day as Jackson, in one over. With MacLaren making a century and Jackson 82 not out, England went on to win by 213 runs. England dominated the second Test, with Jackson taking 4-50, but rain denied them. The third was also drawn with England holding a huge advantage and Jackson scoring 144 not out. He made another century in the fourth Test which England won by an innings – thus becoming the only player to score five centuries against Australia in England. Scores of 76 and 31 in the final drawn Test saw Jackson to the top of both batting and bowling averages in the series – and to a place as national hero. English cricket was at a zenith, but the golden age was already creeping to its end.

Jackson's career virtually ended with the triumph of 1905. He played three matches in 1906, and, in 1907, he appeared in the Roses match at Headingley. He hit six and 35, Yorkshire won by nine wickets, and the first-class career of the greatest all-rounder of the greatest period in the history of English cricket was at an end. He had played in 19 Test matches, all against Australia, hit five centuries, scored 1,415 runs at an average of 48.79 and taken 24 wickets at 33.29 although he had bowled only a handful of overs in three series. The career averages show his bowling skills in a truer light – 774 wickets at 20.37. Batting he scored nearly 16,000 runs, average 33.83, with 31 centuries.

Jackson was asked to take the England side to Australia in 1907 and again to lead England in 1909, but he declined on both occasions 'owing to pressure of business'. The family firm occupied him much, but Lord Allerton realised that neither of his sons was anxious to take on the whole burden of the business and, in 1913, four years before his death, he sold it to the Laycock brothers.

This left Stanley Jackson free to concentrate on his political ambitions. He did not desert cricket altogether. He had appeared for Lords and Commons Cricket, and now played for Old Harrovians, but golf occupied most of his limited leisure time. There is a legend that he had never played golf before spending a winter standing in front of a dressing-room mirror perfecting a swing. When he took a club in his hand the following summer he was a near scratch golfer, and within two years was capable of taking on anyone in the land. Jackson was blessed, at least in sport. In politics, he was to find the going harder.

Within weeks of the outbreak of the First World War, he joined the Territorial Association of the West Riding of Yorkshire. He raised and commanded a battalion of the Leeds Rifles, and, as Lieutenant-Colonel, set sail for France with his battalion in January 1917. His command was short-lived, for he was retired from active service through sickness in March the same year.

Jackson was already a Member of Parliament before he went to France, having been elected for the Howdenshire Division of Yorkshire, the seat previously held by his father-in-law, in the summer of 1915. Deprived of the opportunity to serve at the front, he now threw himself whole-heartedly into the work of an MP and spoke on a variety of subjects in the House. There were many there who were known to him, and it is said that when Winston Churchill introduced him to Lloyd

George in the dining-room of the House of Commons Lloyd George responded gleefully, 'I have been looking all my life for the man who gave Winston Churchill a hiding at school'.

In October 1922, Bonar Law appointed him Financial Secretary to the War Office, but he held the post only until March the following year. 'Jacker' then became chairman of the Conservative and Unionist Party. The appointment was celebrated in the *Daily News Cricket Annual* where it was remembered that he led England in the days when they could beat Australia and that, having reached the summit in the parliament of cricket (he was president of MCC in 1921), he was now about to do the same in politics.

This was not to be the case. Jackson was one of Bonar Law's men, and Bonar Law died in 1923. He was no favourite of Baldwin, despite being a contemporary at Harrow, and he had neither the intellect nor the political acumen to find his way through the pitfalls of Parliament. It was also not the most favourable time in which to be chairman of the party.

Jackson was one of those who persuaded Baldwin to go to the country at the end of 1923 on the issue of Free Trade which, in reversal of Conservative policy, the Prime Minister proposed to abandon in favour of a system of complete Protection. The Conservatives remained the largest party after the election, but Labour, with the promise of Liberal support, was able to form a government. Although Ramsay MacDonald, who acted as Foreign Secretary as well as Prime Minister, made some advances in helping to improve relations between France and Germany, the dependence on Liberal support allowed only meagre domestic legislation, and, in the autumn of 1924, that support was withdrawn. The country was faced with another General Election.

It is most probable the Conservatives would have been returned to power whatever issues were raised, but the affair of the Zinoviev Letter was certain to assure the defeat of the Labour Government. In 1924, a document called the Red Letter was published in the *Daily Mail* and in other papers which supported the Conservative Party. The letter purported to be written by Grigori Zinoviev, chairman of the Communist International, and instructed the British Communist Party on ways of controlling the Labour movement. By inference, it implicated the Labour Party and the Trade Union movement in a conspiracy to overthrow parliamentary democracy.

The authenticity of the document was later virtually discredited, but the damage had been done. Labour lost 42 seats out of 192; the Liberals 119 out of 158; and the Conservatives gained 152. Baldwin was back with a sweeping majority. As chairman of the Conservative Party during the election, Jackson came out of the business badly, his character stained. He was a man of great integrity, but politically naive and even out of his depth.

Baldwin employed Jackson to influence Churchill to return to the Tory benches, and the Prime Minister then appointed Churchill Chancellor of the Exchequer, which bewildered Jackson. He still worked hard to streamline the party organisation, called in a efficiency expert and increased expenditure, none of which made him popular within certain sections of the party. The Conservatives needed reform, but Stanley Jackson was not the man equipped for the task. He had been the best bad wicket batsman in England, but he did not have the technique necessary to cope with ambitious politicians or minor party crises. On the cricket field he had been supreme; in the arena of politics he struggled.

By the end of 1926, Baldwin was pressing for changes, and Jackson stood down. It was the end of his political career. He was knighted and appointed Governor of Bengal. Baldwin had put him on the boat for India before he really grasped what was happening.

He found the problems in Calcutta even more demanding than those he had encountered in running the Conservative Party. Bengal was a turbulent state, and Jackson was trapped between the policies of oppression and liberalism. Eventually, he dissolved the provincial legislature and replaced it with a governing body more acceptable to the Raj. In 1932, shortly before the end of his time in India, he survived an assassination attempt by a young woman graduate in the Senate Hall of the University of Calcutta. Five shots were fired but Jackson was left unscathed, remarking that it was the quickest duck that he had ever made.

Back in England, Jackson, an opponent of leg theory, made attempts to pacify the situation after the body-line affair. He then became chairman of Selectors for the 1934 series against Australia when he had no Jardine nor Larwood to call upon. He became chairman of Yorkshire in succession to his friend Lord Hawke in 1938, and chairman of the Governors of Harrow in 1942. He had led a life which brought him many honours and much acclaim, but the glory days had been spent on the cricket field where his mastery of the orthodox, his temperament and self-belief put him among the great players of all time.

His London house was destroyed in the blitz when he was not at home, but, having survived the war, he was knocked down by a taxi in 1946 and never fully recovered, dying in March 1947. A final tale of this remarkable man. When a disconsolate Len Hutton was surveying his post-war future as a cricketer from his hospital bed, having endured surgery on his left arm, who should emerge but Sir Stanley. Hutton never forgot his kindliness and encouragement that day.

In his time as Governor of Bengal, Jackson had tried to implement the reforms suggested by Lord Chelmsford who had been Viceroy of India from 1916 to 1921 and had succeeded Jackson as president of MCC in 1922. The eldest of five sons of the Second Lord Chelmsford, Frederic John Napier Thesiger was a far better scholar than Stanley Jackson. Educated at Winchester where he gained a reputation as being a hard hitting batsman, he went up to Magdalen College, Oxford, where he took a First in Jurisprudence and was appointed a Fellow of All Souls in 1892.

He was in the Oxford side for four years, gaining his blue as a Freshman in 1888, but, in fact, he only played in two Varsity matches. He hit 26 in his first year, withdrew from the side in his second because of the illness of his brother, scored 0 and 4 in his third, when he was captain and Jackson was in his first year at Cambridge, and, in 1891, he was forced to leave the field after lunch on the first day with a sprained wrist. Gregor MacGregor, the Cambridge captain, sportingly allowed T. B. Case to replace him, and Thesiger's name does not appear on the final scorecard.

Thesiger had played for Worcestershire while still at school, and he made his first appearance for Middlesex after his first Varsity match in 1888. He batted number three against Gloucestershire at Cheltenham and hit 30. Middlesex won by an innings. He was never able to play regularly for the county. Three matches in 1892, his last season, was the most in which he played, and it was in that season that he hit 60 not out against Surrey at The Oval.

The nephew of A. H. Thesiger who had played for MCC in the 1860s, Frederic was called to the Bar in 1893, but he was, by tradition and temperament, drawn to public affairs rather than a professional career. He saw education as vital in a democracy and made a full study of the educational system. From 1900 to 1904, he was a member of the London School Board, and elected to the LCC.

He succeeded to the title in 1905 and was appointed Governor of Queensland, moving in 1909 to become Governor of New South Wales. He was admirably qualified for these positions, not least because he had played first-class cricket, but also as a tall, well-built, handsome, dignified, sociable and easy mannered figure. His tact and charm did much to lighten the task of the first Labour Government for New South Wales in 1910.

Returning to England at the outbreak of the First World War, he became a Captain in the Fourth Dorset Territorials and went with his regiment to India where he saw no fighting. In 1916, he was appointed Viceroy of India – an unexpected choice for this important post. He was only 47 and perhaps too inexperienced for so difficult a task in time of war. The mismanagement of the campaign in Mesopotamia had not eased the British task of ruling India – tragically, Chelmsford was to lose his eldest son in Mesopotamia within a year of his appointment in India – and there was a growing demand for constitutional advance as well as violence in Bengal.

Chelmsford recognised the need for more self-government and, in

July 1917, a policy for India was defined which spoke of 'the progressive realisation of responsible government'. This led to the Government of India Act in 1919 which set India on the path to Home Rule. But for Chelmsford, problems multiplied. Gandhi launched his campaign of passive resistance; there was murderous disorder in the Punjab; and the Third Afghan War broke out.

Lord Chelmsford's main link with India had been that his mother came from a family closely linked with the Indian army; now he had a crisis to overcome. This was mastered, but it left behind the shadow of Amritsar, the massacre of Indian civilians at the order of Brigadier-General R. E. H. Dyer. Dyer was eventually censured by the Government of India, but there was a long delay in conducting an inquiry into the tragedy, and for that, Chelmsford was to take the blame.

In 1921, back in England, he resumed his interest in education and was chairman of the Committee of University College, London, and of the commission appointed in 1923 to revise the statutes of Oxford University. In 1924, he accepted the invitation to become First Lord of the Admiralty in Ramsay MacDonald's First Labour Government.

In essence, this was an appointment even more surprising than the one that had taken Chelmsford to India. The formation of that First Labour Government was considered with trepidation by many from Buckingham Palace downwards for it was all based on the support of Asquith and the Liberals, and Labour had no experience of government. From the start, MacDonald's hands were tied, and it was generally believed that Chelmsford's appointment owed much to a violent protest by senior naval officers that they would not accept a Socialist in the position. Chelmsford was not a member of the Labour Party, and he thought that 13 years of neutrality overseas had freed him from party ties. He believed as regards the navy directly and India indirectly that his inclusion in the Cabinet would strengthen public confidence, but he did not have the chance to prove himself in either administration or debate. The government lasted only ten months, and Chelmsford left no mark from his tenure of office.

In 1929, he again became a Fellow of All Souls, and in 1932, its Warden. He was warmly liked and respected, but he was not to enjoy his high position at his old university for long. In April 1933, he suffered a sudden and fatal heart attack.

Many honours had been showered upon him – he was made a Viscount on his return from India by which time he was already a Privy Councillor and the recipient of the KCMG and the GCMG He was given many honorary degrees and was generally popular, but, ultimately, he was an academic who fulfilled himself neither as a cricketer nor as a politician.

Cricket and The Question of India

INDIA claims a strange hold on cricketing politicians: Lord Harris; Stanley Jackson who gave Ranjitsinhji his blue at Cambridge; Lord Chelmsford; and Lord Willingdon for whom, perhaps, cricket and politics were to become inextricably blended.

Born Freeman Thomas, the son of Freeman Frederick Thomas who played nine matches for Sussex in the 1860s, took the name Freeman Freeman-Thomas in 1892 and was created the First Lord Willingdon in 1910. He was in the Eton XI for three seasons, being captain in 1885 and winning his blue as a Freshman at Cambridge the following year. He was in the light blues side for four years and although he did nothing spectacular in the Varsity matches, hit a fine 114 against Yorkshire in June 1887, topping the university batting averages that season.

He made 18 appearances for Sussex between 1886 and 1890 but before he was elected Liberal MP for Hastings in 1890, his first-class cricket in England had ceased – 40 matches with an average of 23.00. From 1906 to 1910, he was MP for Bodmin, and then president of Sussex in 1911 by which time he had become Lord Willingdon.

Willingdon joined Lord Loreburn in Asquith's Liberal Government in 1911 as Junior Lord to the Treasury, but his real destiny was for politics abroad. From 1913 to 1918, he was Governor of Bombay, and from 1919 to 1924 Governor of Madras. He became Governor General of Canada and, in 1931, he returned to India as Viceroy.

Lord Willingdon is a paradox. Where Chelmsford and Irwin had approached the nationalist movement with attempts at dialogue and negotiation, Willingdon adopted a tough line which saw Gandhi imprisoned and a general policy crushing any display of dissent to British rule. In his own words, he was a dictator, yet he began to play a prominent role in the development of Indian cricket at home and abroad.

In his first periods in India, Willingdon had organised matches in Bombay and Madras, fielding his own XI, and, in November 1918, at the age of 51, captaining England against India. The England side included Harry Lee (the Middlesex opener), Gerry Weigall, J. S. Heath of Derbyshire, and the Hampshire pair John Newman and W.H. Livsey. There were 12 on each side, and England avoided a crushing innings defeat only with the last pair together. More importantly, Willingdon's clubs in Bombay and Madras, unlike the English clubs, were open to all, and he made every effort to field sides which contained both Europeans and Indians of all creeds.

When he returned to India in 1931 Willingdon found Indian cricket in a sorry state, desperately in need of leadership and direction. He threw himself into the power struggle with a passion that rivalled Warwick the Kingmaker.

As Mihir Bose has stated in his admirable *History of Indian Cricket*, Ranjitsinhji would have been the obvious choice as leader of Indian cricket, but he wanted no part in it. He even forbade his nephew, Duleepsinhji, to play for India. This had happened before Willingdon's return to India, but the bitter reverberations were still apparent. The void left by the attitudes of Ranjitsinhji and his nephew created the fight for control of cricket in India between rival princes.

To Willingdon, cricket was important, not only because he loved the game and had been a most capable player but also because he recognised it as the vital link between the Indians and the British. He had the greatest concern as to who would emerge as leader of the game in India both for political and cricketing reasons.

The Maharajah of Patiala had been seen as the most likely man to lead, for he had played a big part in helping to form the Cricket Board of India. There was, however, scandal attached to his name and Willingdon did not like him, considering him to be a fool. Patiala's main rival for the leadership came from an unexpected source, the Maharajkumar of Vizianagram, who had shown considerable political awareness when he organised a team of his own to tour India and Ceylon in 1930-31 after an MCC tour of the country had been cancelled due to political unrest. Not only did he gather the best of Indian cricketers to his side, but he also persuaded the mighty Hobbs and Sutcliffe to play for him. It was a master stroke, and together with Vizianagram's offer to subsidise, in part at least, India's coming tour of England, 1932, it cemented his alliance with Willingdon.

Vizianagram had ambitions to become captain of India, but there was a faction which believed that no Indian was capable of leading the national side and welding the varied talents and religions into a unit. Willingdon made no secret of the fact that this was his opinion. He saw the wider political issues and felt that if an Englishman captained India, it would symbolise that the British rule in the country was needed. If the British left India, the country would collapse into chaos, unable to administer itself.

Patiala, however, was to outmanoeuvre both Vizianagram and Willingdon. He played his trump card at the meeting of the Board when he offered to stage the trials from which the side to tour England would be chosen and to meet all the expenses for the whole month. He had made an offer that could not be refused. No Europeans were invited to the trials. Vizianagram was beaten, and Willingdon could only mutter disapproval. When the side was named Patiala was captain, Prince Gyanashyamsinhji of Limbdi was vice-captain, and Vizianagram was offered the post of deputy vice-captain. He refused due to 'pressures of state'.

Patiala had not intended to captain the party to England and stood down in favour of the Maharajah of Porbander. The new captain was certainly not a cricketer of ability. In four first-class matches in England, he averaged 0.66 with a highest score of two. Limbdi was better, but well below Test standard, and in the inaugural Test match at Lord's, C. K. Nayudu was captain in spite of his lack of royal pedigree. He was an excellent cricketer but suffered from political intrigue.

Willingdon crushed Gandhi's civil disobedience movement with harsh measures, and in the debates which followed regarding the future of India, the Chamber of Princes found itself with slightly increased powers although not ones which would lead to independence. In any case, the princes were not nationalists.

On the death of Ranjitsinhji in 1933, Patiala was elected Chancellor of the Chamber of Princes, far from the liking of Willingdon who still considered him as an unreliable fool. But as Patiala's political power seemed to increase, his power in cricket politics declined. On the eve of the MCC's first Test tour of England, 1933-34, the Board of Control was divided into three zones each of which was to nominate a selector. Only the West forwarded an Indian representative.

Patiala was as yet unbowed. He wanted his son Yuvraj, who had some talent and had been well coached, to captain India. He lavished hospitality on Jardine's side, and, to the fury of Willingdon, Patiala himself played for MCC, but Nayudu led India in the Tests. In the first Test, he shared a stand of 186 with Amarnath who made India's initial century in a Test match. More will be said of Amarnath later. Yuvraj played his one and only Test in the third Madras match of the series, acquitting himself well with a top score of 60 in India's second innings of 249.

Not only was the Indian side for the series selected by two Englishmen, but the umpires were the Englishmen Hitch and Higgins, and the Australian, Tarrant, to whom Jardine objected after two Tests. Tarrant was a Patiala man, who heartened by his son's performance on a turning wicket at Madras, made further claims to lead Indian cricket and install Yuvraj as captain.

He first provided the money to cover losses after the MCC tour. This gave him a firmer grip on the Board of Control to whom he now proposed donating a trophy for a national domestic competition of India. It was to be called the Ranji Trophy in honour of the great Ranjitsinhji despite having done little for cricket in his native country. Vizianagram seized upon this fact and suggested that a more appropriate name for such a trophy would be the Willingdon Trophy in honour of the man who had achieved and was still doing so for cricket in India. He even had the trophy made in England to a design by Lady Willingdon.

The competition was already under way, and, in the end, Lord Willingdon presented the Ranji Trophy and not the one that bore his name to the winners, Bombay. Patiala now seemed supreme in Indian cricket but at his height he became vulnerable. Using his disciple Frank Tarrant, he brought a non-Test team of Australians to India, 1935-36. His former ADC, Colonel Mistry, was named as manager for the tour of England, 1936, with Duleepsinhji, the Nawab of Pataudi and Dr Kanga appointed selectors. The Willingdon influence, it seemed, had been countered.

Vizianagram responded by staging a Silver Jubilee Festival in honour of King George V, when his team won the competition and the Willingdon Trophy. Carefully manipulating affairs during the Australian tour, Vizianagram first accounted for the Nawab of Pataudi's claim on the captaincy of India because of health reasons, allowed Yuvraj to disqualify himself through unpopularity to such an extent that his father withdrew his candidature. He then hinted that Nayudu was the cause of all the troubles so that others would not serve under him. This left only Vizianagram himself as the man to captain India in England in 1936.

The victory of Willingdon, through Vizianagram, was complete. Vizianagram had the captaincy he so desired; Willingdon had beaten Patiala. To compound the victory, Captain R. J. Brittain-Jones, the Comptroller of the Viceroy's Household, was now chosen as manager instead of the previously named Patiala man, Colonel Mistry. The significance of this change was to be learned all too strongly in the weeks ahead.

It must first be stated that Vizianagram, who was feted during the tour and knighted in between the first and second Tests, was barely of first-class standard. In the words of Edward Docker, an historian of Indian cricket: 'If only he could have played the game as well as he looked the part. But he was no cricketer, however much people in Britain tried to pretend that he was, even though his aggregate of runs at the end of the tour was 600, an average of 16.21 per innings. "What did he expect me to do?" an English county captain complained after 'Vizzy' had presented him with a gold watch just before their match began. "I gave him a full toss and a couple of long hops, but you can't go on bowling like that all day, not in England."'

His average in the three Tests was 8.25, and he lacked the qualities needed to captain a cricket team – the manipulation of bowlers, the setting of fields, and the intelligent use of batting resources. In fairness, with the team divided into factions and a majority of them believing that only Nayudu should lead the side, Vizianagram's task was never going to be an easy one, particularly as he and Nayudu were scarcely on speaking terms. Vizianagram was captain without a deputy and sole selector, along with Captain Brittain-Jones.

Strains appeared early in the tour. At Leicester, Amarnath who, since scoring India's first century in Test cricket, was a national hero, had a bitter altercation with his captain about field-placings and had been warned as to his 'attitude towards the captain and manager'. He was the outstanding player in those early weeks, hitting a century against Northamptonshire, a century in each innings against Essex and taking wickets regularly.

His batting had slumped a little. He felt he needed practice, but rain interrupted the match against Minor Counties at Lord's and Merchant and Mushtaq Ali shared a double century partnership. This meant that Amarnath, due to bat at number four, was padded up and waiting impatiently for a long time. Vizianagram then came to him and told him that he was not going in next as other batsmen needed the practice more. He finally batted at number seven with only a few minutes left.

He stormed off the field at the close, flung his bat and pads into a corner of the dressing-room and loudly condemned the whole way in which the side was being led and the way he was being treated. He also abused one of the entourage who tried to inquire if and when players wanted a massage. Unfortunately for Amarnath, the commotion disturbed the members in the room below the Indian dressing-room, and it is possible that Lord Willingdon was one of those affected.

At 6pm the following evening, the Friday, Amarnath was summoned by Brittain-Jones and ordered to return to India the next morning. C. K. Nayudu, Wazir Ali and other senior members of the side pleaded on behalf of Amarnath. A letter of apology was drafted and given to Vizianagram who agreed to rescind the order, but the captain did not have the power. Brittain-Jones (and Willingdon) had made the decision and to change it would have been a sign of political weakness. On the Saturday morning, Amarnath was on his way back to India, and a side that was never a strong one was seriously weakened by the loss of its leading all-rounder.

The Board of Control was never offered an explanation, and when Amarnath arrived in India they asked if they could send him back to England to rejoin the party. Brittain-Jones and Vizianagram refused. Even while Amarnath was returning to India, Lord Willingdon spoke at a dinner at The Oval, condemning the all-rounder and supporting the captain and manager to both of whom, in effect, he gave orders.

Vizianagram returned to India ahead of his team at the end of the tour in an attempt to halt an inquiry that was being set up. He failed, and Amarnath, later to become a captain of India and a chairman of selectors, was exonerated. For a time, Vizianagram was out of favour in cricket circles, but he was to return in the post war period and to hold high and influential offices. He had learned much from Willingdon and was, in any case, a clever politician in his own right, becoming a member of the Indian Parliament.

Lord Willingdon's term as Viceroy of India ended in 1936 when he returned to England. He died at Westminster in 1941 a month before his 75th birthday. He had attempted to rule Indian cricket with the same rod of iron with which he carried out his viceregal duties. His name will not be forgotten in India where he made his mark in cricket and politics, and for much of the time the two were indistinguishable.

It seems that fate drew cricketing politicians to India for the twilight of their careers. As an example, Arthur Oswald James Hope found his last post there. He was from a military family and he married into a military family. Educated at Oratory School he then moved on to Sandhurst before joining the Coldstream Guards in 1914.

The future Second Baron Rankeillour served with distinction in France from 1915 to 1919. Severely wounded, he won the Military Cross, was Mentioned in Despatches and was awarded the Croix de Guerre. He served in Turkey in 1922 and 1923, and then he turned his attention to politics.

At the November election, 1924, he became Conservative MP for the Nuneaton Division of Warwickshire, holding the seat until 1929. For the first two years of this period, he was Parliamentary Private Secretary to Colonel G. R. Lane Fox, the Secretary for Mines, and, in 1926, he played his one and only game of first-class cricket – for the Army against Cambridge University at Fenner's when he batted at number three and scored 2 and 23. According to *Wisden*, 'Neither side was strongly represented', and Cambridge, who did have E. W. Dawson, R. A. Ingle, M. J. Turnbull, H. J. Enthoven, E. F. Longrigg, Walter Robins and Maurice Allom in their side, won in two days.

Lord Home played with Hope and described him as 'a very competent left-hand batsman who would have made a solid number four in any club side.' He was certainly a tower of strength in Lords and Commons Cricket, averaging 31 in his 12 innings against MCC in the matches played between 1924 and 1939. Nobody else batted as much during that period, and he was ever willing to appear in any kind of parliamentary game.

The 1931 General Election swept the Government from office and virtually obliterated the Parliamentary Labour Party. It also brought

Hope back to Parliament as Unionist Member for the Aston Division of Birmingham, when he became part of a Nationalist Government that had a majority of 500. He was to feel little financial benefit from this for, although he was Assistant Whip in 1935 and Junior Lord of the Treasury from 1935 to 1937, he received no payment for either of these posts.

From May to October 1937, the months immediately following the coronation of George VI, he was Vice-Chamberlain of HM Household, and from the October until the outbreak of war, he was Treasurer of HM Household. The Second World War was spent in India. In 1940, he became Governor of Madras, always it seems a cricketer's position, and he remained in that post until 1946 when great changes began to take place on the sub-continent.

The three main passions of his life were hunting, shooting and cricket which he loved with an undying fervour. It must have given great pleasure that his Madras Governor's XI beat the strong Madras provincial side at Christmas, 1941, with future stars like V. S. Hazare and H. R. Adhikari in his side.

Like A. O. J. Hope, Lord Kenneth Augustus Muir-Mackenzie appeared in only one first-class cricket match, and again like Rankeillour, his Government post was as a Whip, being Lord in Waiting in the first Labour administration in 1924 and again occupying the post in Ramsay MacDonald's Second Ministry in 1929. Muir-Mackenzie died in May 1930, while in office. He was 85, and his had been a life time of service.

A barrister by profession, he had been Warden of Winchester College from 1904 to 1915. A member of the Royal Commission on the Civil Service, Permanent Principal Secretary to the Lord Chancellor and Clerk to the Crown in Chancery for 35 years, he was the son-in-law of W. Graham who had been MP for Glasgow in the 19th century. He was sworn in as a Privy Councillor when he took office under Ramsay MacDonald in 1924, and he had been knighted in 1898.

What is remarkable is that Muir-Mackenzie seemed to have left his sporting interests so far in the past. He was educated at Charterhouse and Balliol College, Oxford, and at Charterhouse he had been captain of the cricket and soccer sides. Yet his one first-class match was for MCC against Oxford University, at Lord's in June 1870, when he was 25. Oxford made 114, and MCC were 74-6 when Muir-Mackenzie joined W. G. Grace. Muir-Mackenzie scored 17, and the pair added 35. No doubt it was because of this success that he was promoted to open with Grace in the second innings. This time he made four, and his first-class career was at an end.

So, seemingly, was his serious interest in the game. In spite of being a member of MCC, he did not list cricket among his recreations, and his passing was not remarked upon by the cricket press. In politics, he seems to have been one of those who avoided the question of India which Willingdon has allowed us to do at more than balanced length.

Charles Lennox *(above)*, the Fourth Duke of Richmond, was one of those natural talents and a supreme athlete. He ran, and he jumped, but, above all, he played cricket, being an outstanding batsman and wicketkeeper for two decades.

William Ward's success in business was mirrored by his prowess as a sportsman. He supported Thomas Lord in his endeavours to establish a ground, and when the third, last and most famous of Lord's grounds came into being in 1814, Ward *(right)*, played in the inaugural 'great' match at the new venue.

George Osbaldeston *(above)*, famously described as the 'Squire of England', was as commanding an all-round figure as the Fourth Duke of Richmond. He was a great gambler whose single-wicket match challenge to the Revd Lord Frederick Beauclerk aroused still more public interest than a pistol duel between the two at Wormword Scrubs.

William Nicholson (*left*), one of the few presidents of MCC in the 19th century not born into the aristocracy, scored his runs very quickly and was 'one of the best wicketkeepers in England'. He played for Middlesex sides before the county club came into being, and for county club itself against MCC in its first season and against Hampshire the following year.

Alfred Lyttelton (*right*), touched everything to which he turned his hand with brilliance. An England cricket and soccer international, he was a safe and quick wicketkeeper who claimed 134 catches and 70 stumpings in his 101 first-class matches. The highest of his seven centuries was for Middlesex against Gloucestershire, at Clifton, in 1883.

Sir Stanley Jackson is on paper the best all-rounder in both spheres. One of the most effective cricketing performers, particularly in a crisis, he was, however, far less influential in his various party posts. He won all the honours the world of cricket has to give, however.

Lord Harris captained England and also led Kent until 1889 when his political duties forced him to stand down. At the age of 60 years 5 months, he remains the oldest man to appear in a first-class match in England. He played good club cricket, scoring runs in his 60s and 70s and was 73 when, as captain of Lords and Commons, he saved the match against MCC by batting for an hour.

Son of a Prime Minister, Lord Dalmeny – later the Sixth Earl of Rosebery – captained Surrey from 1905 to 1907 when pressure of business and politics forced him to stand down. He was Liberal Member for Midlothian from 1906 to 1910, so here was a working MP at the wicket. In his first season as captain, he hit centuries against Leicestershire and Warwickshire and reached 1,000 runs, as he did in his last season.

The First Lord Willingdon – born Freeman Thomas – was in the Cambridge side for four years and hit 114 against Yorkshire in June 1887, topping the university batting averages that season. He made 18 appearances for Sussex between 1886 and 1890 but before he was elected Liberal MP for Hastings in 1890, his first-class cricket in England had ceased – 40 matches with an average of 23.00. From 1906 to 1910, he was MP for Bodmin, and then president of Sussex in 1911.

The Maharajah of Patiala had been seen as the most likely man to lead Indian cricket out of its mess for he had played a big part in helping to form the Cricket Board of India. There was, however, scandal attached to his name and Lord Willingdon did not like him, considering him to be a fool.

Lionel Tennyson's story is the stuff of legends. He played 347 matches for Hampshire until retirement, captaining them with vigour from 1919-1933. After a distinguished military career in the First World War – twice wounded and twice mentioned in despatches – Tennyson showed his Rifle Brigade courage yet again when playing for England in 1921. Here he is pictured going out to inspect the wicket at The Oval. Australian skipper Warwick Armstrong refused to join him, declaring the crowd too hostile.

Sir Samuel Hill-Wood captained Derbyshire from 1899 to 1901 and was the Conservative Member for High Peak for 19 years after election in 1910. Sir Samuel was one of the most prominent figures in sport in the first half of the century. Most significantly he was chairman of Arsenal FC from 1927 until his death in 1949. Here he is talking to the Gunners' Archie Macaulay after victory over Bolton Wanderers at Highbury in 1947.

Sir Walter Monckton *(left)*, made his one first-class appearance for a combined Oxford and Cambridge side against a combined Army and Navy side at Portsmouth in 1911. Not out in his first innings, batting at number 11, he has the highly respectable batting average in first-class cricket of 72. He is pictured here as Minister of Labour and National Service in 1953.

Hubert Ashton *(right)*, played a significant part in the famous victory by Archie MacLaren's all-amateur side over the Australians at Eastbourne in 1921. Ashton was an outstanding sportsman who might have led English cricket out of the doldrums, but when he came down from university, he went to Burma and apart from occasional appearances for Essex when on leave, was lost to English cricket. Hugh Gaitskill's brother-in-law, he was he was elected to Parliament in 1950.

Michael Falcon's bowling helped give Archie MacLaren's side victory at Eastbourne in 1921 against the hitherto all-conquering Australian visitors. Falcon's record in first-class cricket suggests that if he had given himself fully to the game, he would have been an outstanding player. Although he did not play for a first-class county he was chosen for the Gentlemen against the Players ten times between 1911 and 1927. In 1918, he was elected Unionist Member for East Norfolk, but lost his seat in 1923 and did not venture into politics again.

Prime Minister Stanley Baldwin was later MCC president and had a son-in-law who was a fine cricketer. But he was perhaps most proud of his wife, the former Lucy Ridsdale, who in 1892 averaged 62 with the bat while playing for the White Heather ladies' club. Her father was a high ranking officer at the Royal Mint responsible for determining the amount of gold or silver in coins. Here Mr and Mrs Baldwin are pictured after voting at Caxton Hall in November 1935.

Lord Home going out to bat for Lords and Commons at The Oval in 1951. In 1924, as Lord Dunglass, he made his first-class debut for Middlesex and when he became Prime Minister in September 1963, Sir Alec Douglas-Home was the first incumbent of No 10 Downing Street ever to have played first-class cricket. His career of ten first-class matches matches, yielded 147 runs, average 16.33. He made eight catches and took 12 wickets for 363 runs. He also toured South America with an MCC side in 1926-27.

Aiden Crawley was a first-class cricketer, fighter pilot, escaped PoW, Member of Parliament, journalist and documentary film maker among other things. A member of a fine cricketing family, he played for Oxford and for Kent and in his first-class career, which also encompassed games for Free Foresters, scored 5,061 runs with 11 centuries and an average of 37.48. At different times he represented the Buckingham Division of North Buckinghamshire and West Derbyshire for Labour and Conservative respectively.

The Revd David Sheppard strikes a four during the second day's play in the final Test against New Zealand in March 1963. He captained Sussex and England and his first-class career saw him play in 22 Tests with 3 centuries at an average of 37.80 and a first-class total of 15,838 runs in 230 matches at 43.51. David Sheppard's ecclesiastical following took him from Bishop Suffragan of Woolwich to Bishop of Liverpool. The Life Peerage – for Labour – came in 1998.

England captain Colin Cowdrey tosses a coin watched by West Indies skipper Garfield Sobers. In 114 Tests, Cowdrey was captain 27 times, finishing with an average of 44.06 with 22 centuries. His 120 catches beat the then Hammond Test record for a non wicketkeeper. Cowdrey's county career had several peaks – notably Kent winning a championship in their centenary year. His first-class career saw an average of 42.89 in 692 matches with 107 centuries and 638 catches. President of MCC in their bicentenary year, he was chairman of the ICC 1989-93 and was created a Conservative Life Peer in 1997 – Lord Cowdrey of Tonbridge.

Gentlemen and Eccentrics Between the Acts

IN THE summer of 1921, the Australians, under Warwick Armstrong, completed their eighth Test victory in succession over England. The last two Tests of the five-match series were drawn, mainly through Australian apathy, and when Armstrong's side arrived at Eastbourne at the end of August for their 35th game of the tour they had 19 victories and 14 draws behind them. Throughout the miseries that English cricket suffered that summer Archie MacLaren had boasted that he could field a side that would beat these all-conquering Australians. The match at Eastbourne saw his claim put to the test.

Archie MacLaren, for whom Winston Churchill had fagged at Harrow, was nearly 50. An eccentric of great charisma, he had a poor record as captain of England. The team he gathered together to play Armstrong's Australians was entirely amateur. He captained a side which included three Ashton brothers, Percy Chapman, Aubrey

Faulkner, C. H. Gibson, Walter Brearley (a rebellious spirit, 45 years old with his first-class career ten years in the past), G. N. Foster, wicketkeeper G. E. C. Wood and Michael Falcon.

MacLaren won the toss, and, on a wicket which offered bowlers no encouragement, his side was bowled out for 43 in 65 minutes. Falcon and Faulkner lessened some of the embarrassment but the visitors still led by 131 on the first innings. When MacLaren's XI were reduced to 60-4 in their second innings it seemed that an early finish was certain, but the South African Aubrey Faulkner was joined by Hubert Ashton, and the pair added 154. Faulkner went on to make 153, and the Australians were left to score 196 to win the match.

This appeared to be no great problem, but Gibson, in particular, Falcon and Faulkner bowled with such control and aggression that Armstrong's side were dismissed for 167. MacLaren's boast was proved by a margin of 28 runs. This victory was unreported in any newspaper save the *Manchester Guardian* for whose correspondent, Neville Cardus, it was a poetic scoop. He lyricised on this win by a team led by a former Lancashire captain, and the victory passed into folk-lore, taking on a significance far beyond its true worth. The Australians were to win two more matches and then lose their last, in another festival atmosphere, at Scarborough. The hard work was long behind them, and they were unlikely to take these defeats in the closing weeks of their tour too seriously.

In 1921, MacLaren's side was deified by Cardus' eloquent prose. Brearley and MacLaren himself apart, they were young – amateurs shot with romance. Gibson, who took 6-64 in the Australians' second innings, toured New Zealand a year later and then he became lost to England as his work took him to South America. Chapman became the golden boy of English cricket, leading his country out of the wilderness before his sad, personal decline. Wood had been a captain of Cambridge and was to play in three Tests for England against South Africa although his county career was restricted to 41 matches for Kent in eight years. Claude and Gilbert Ashton, too, could give little time to county cricket, and Michael Falcon was to spend his days with Norfolk.

It is to Falcon and to Hubert Ashton – both Parliamentarians – that we should now turn our attention, having given us the opportunity of describing this unique game in the first place.

In the edition that followed the England traumas of 1921, *Wisden* named three Australians among their Five Cricketers of the Year. The two Englishmen were J. L. Bryan and Hubert Ashton who was in his second year at Cambridge.

Ashton's uncles, Alfred and John Inglis, had played for Kent towards the end of the 19th century, and three of his brothers, Claude, Gilbert and Percy appeared in first-class cricket. He was born in Calcutta and played much cricket at a private school in Blackheath before going to Winchester where he had a fine record and captained the XI in 1916, succeeding his brother Gilbert in the post.

In April 1917, he was commissioned in the Royal Field Artillery and sailed for France. He rose to the rank of lieutenant and won the Military Cross. Not demobilised until August 1919, his first-class cricket career could not begin until 1920. Having gone up to Trinity College, Cambridge, he won his blue as a Freshman although he did not secure his place until the end of June when he hit 236 not out against Free Foresters at Fenner's. The visitors attack included Falcon and C. U. Peat of whom more will be heard later.

Ashton's double century against the Free Foresters was to remain the highest score of his career. He also hit a century against Levenson-Gower's XI and topped the Cambridge batting averages. He failed in the Varsity match, but he was selected for the Gentlemen at Lord's. Seemingly, an illustrious career had been launched. Whenever he played against Armstrong's Australians in 1921 he was successful. For Cambridge, he was forced to retire hurt against them, but not until he had made 107, the first century scored against the tourists that season. In six innings against them, he averaged over 58, and most believed that in a season when England caps were liberally sprinkled, one should have gone to Hubert Ashton.

Hubert succeeded his brother Gilbert as captain of Cambridge in 1922, when for the third year in succession he was top of the university batting averages. Seven of his eight first-class centuries were scored for Cambridge, yet the innings by which he was to be remembered for the rest of his life and which was to be forwarded frequently as to the reason that he should have played for England was his 75 for MacLaren's England XI at Eastbourne, in 1921.

A family home in Ingatestone gave Hubert Ashton a residential qualification for Essex. He first appeared for the county in 1921 and he was last to play for them in 1939, but he appeared in only 21 matches in all of that time.

Ashton was a sportsman of outstanding all-round ability. He won blues for soccer and hockey as well as for cricket, and he played soccer for Clapton Orient, Bristol Rovers and for the great Corinthian side of the period. He had all the attributes which were needed to lead English cricket out of the doldrums, but when in 1922 he came down from university, he went to Burma where he was eight years on the staff of the Burmah Oil Company. Apart from occasional appearances for Essex when on leave, he was lost to English cricket.

On one such leave, in 1927, he scored over 300 runs for Essex, and he married Dorothy Margaret Gaitskell, sister of the future Leader of the Labour Party, so indicating his first link with politics. It was not, however, the link with the party with which he was to become associated.

In 1930, he returned to England to take up a senior executive position in the London office of the Burmah Oil Company, and in 1936 became an underwriter at Lloyd's. Even after his return, Hubert Ashton was rarely able to assist Essex, yet, in spite of this, those close to events insist that he was offered the captaincy of the England side to tour Australia, 1932-33. He declined on business grounds, and Jardine was eventually named. The romance of that innings of 75 against Armstrong's Australians was never to be obliterated.

Ashton's association with Burmah Oil lasted until the end of the Second World War. It was then that he turned his attention to farming at Ingatestone, and to politics. He was Deputy Lieutenant of Essex from 1942 until 1978, and in 1946, he was elected County Councillor for

Brentwood (North). Re-elected in April 1949, with an increased majority, he was appointed Vice-chairman of the County Council and made a County Alderman.

These offices were resigned when he was elected to Parliament in 1950. Ashton had fought the seat of the Chelmsford Division of Essex at the General Election of 1945 on behalf of the Conservative Party, but, in the Labour landslide, he had been beaten by the Common Wealth candidate, Wing Commander Millington. At the election in February 1950, there was a straight fight for the seat between Ashton and Millington, and this time Ashton won by 4,859 votes. He held the seat for 14 years so that he found his brother-in-law Hugh Gaitskell always on the benches opposite, ultimately, until his untimely death, as Leader of the Opposition in 1961.

Hubert Ashton became closely associated with another Essex MP, R. A. Butler. He was Parliamentary Private Secretary to Butler when he was first Chancellor of the Exchequer and later Lord Privy Seal and Home Secretary. These parliamentary activities did not preclude him from life outside the House of Commons. He was chairman of Essex CCC, 1946-51, and president from 1949-70. He was also president of MCC in 1960. A strong churchman, he was Church Warden of St Peter's, South Weald, and a Third Church Estates Commissioner at the time of his death in 1979 when he was 81. Had he lived another month he would have seen Essex, whom he had served so well in an administrative capacity, win their first trophy.

Ashton maintained a lively interest in cricket until the end of his life, but when Lord Orr-Ewing tried to persuade him to play for Lords and Commons Cricket shortly after he had been elected to Parliament he declined, saying that whereas he could make runs by instinct, he was no longer adept in the field. A first-class career average of 38.70 in 71 games, and 72 catches, showed his earlier mettle.

Michael Falcon, on the other hand, played for Lords and Commons Cricket against MCC when he was 50, some 15 years after he had lost his seat in Parliament. If Hubert Ashton's talents as a cricketer have tended to be exaggerated because of his 75 for MacLaren's side and his deeds in three years at Cambridge, Falcon has a record in first-class cricket which suggests that if he had given himself fully to the game, he would have been an outstanding player. As it was, he chose to play his cricket for his beloved Norfolk, a decision which almost certainly cost him international recognition.

He was in the XI at Harrow in 1906 and 1907, winning his blue in each of his four years at Cambridge. He had bowled little at Harrow and practically not at all at Cambridge until his last year, 1911, when he took 34 wickets. Falcon had been captain of the side in 1910, impressing all shrewd observers with his pace, late away swing and control. He was also a most capable batsman and a brilliant fielder. Although he did not play for a first-class county, he was chosen to represent the Gentlemen against the Players ten times between 1911 and 1927.

Falcon began by capturing the wickets of Wilfred Rhodes, J. T. Tyldesley and Philip Mead at a personal cost of 87 runs at Scarborough in 1911 when he also hit 75, and ended by taking 4-60 at The Oval in 1927. At The Oval in 1913, he performed magnificently to take 6-58, when Pelham Warner was much criticised for not bowling him more and sooner. In 1924, at The Oval, he took 7-78, including the wickets of Hobbs and Woolley, and then shared a last-wicket stand of 134 in an hour with Arthur Gilligan.

It seemed that Michael Falcon could always rise to the big occasion, and there were many who thought he should have played in the Test series of 1921 when England were desperately in need of a quick bowler. When he captured six Australian wickets for 67 runs in the first innings of that famous match at Eastbourne, people were convinced that a grave error of non-selection had been committed. He might even have been chosen five years later when at the age of 38, with a shortened run and moderated pace, he welcomed the Australians with figures of 7-42 at Holyport. His final first-class match was to come in 1936, for Free Foresters against Cambridge University.

It should be emphasised that this was not the end of Falcon's cricket. He had first played for Norfolk in 1906, at the age of 18, and he captained the county from 1912 to 1946. He was 58 when he last played, and no longer bowled, but he still scored more runs than anyone else in the side and was top of the batting averages. Altogether he scored more than 11,000 runs for Norfolk with 727 wickets at 16.13 apiece as a bonus. He took 231 wickets in his limited first-class career and hit four centuries (average 25.24 in 89 matches), but chose to play for the county of his birth and among the people he knew and loved.

The political career was more brief. A quiet, modest man, Falcon went into the legal profession when he left Pembroke College, and it was as a barrister in Norfolk that he spent his days, living close to Norwich Cathedral. In 1918, he was elected Unionist Member of Parliament for East Norfolk, but lost his seat in 1923 and did not venture into politics again although he maintained his friendships with many in Parliament.

Nothing gave him greater pleasure in his last years than encouraging the young. Chesterton and Doggart wrote of him, 'When he presented the caps at Norwich to the English Schools Under-15 side in 1971 – five years before his death – he was the same courteous and friendly person that his contemporaries had known.'

When Falcon lost his seat in 1923 and until the arrival of Aidan Crawley in 1945 there was only one Blue in the House of Commons, Charles Urie Peat who came in as Unionist Member for Darlington in 1931 when the National Government was swept to power with a majority of 500.

As a cricketer with first-class experience, Peat was immediately pressed into service for Lords and Commons Cricket, but he had not played in a first-class game since 1922 when he had opened the bowling for Free Foresters against Oxford University. His career, in effect, had been brought to a stop by the First World War.

Born in Edmonton in 1892, he was educated at Sedbergh and went on to Oxford. A right-arm fast bowler, he won his place in the university side as a senior in 1913, taking 6-51 (including three wickets in four balls) in his first match for the dark blues, against a strong side got together by H. K. Foster. This proved to be the best performance of his brief career, and he finished the season with 27 wickets and his blue.

The following season Peat played for Middlesex in the two matches against the universities and in four championship games. He took ten wickets and showed good promise, but war broke out on 4 August, and that marked the end of his county career.

Like Falcon, he served throughout the First World War, from 1914 to 1919, winning the Military Cross. In the 1920s, he was fully occupied with his work as a chartered accountant, and it was not until 1931 that politics played a major part in his life. He held the Darlington seat for 14 years, but it was not until the outbreak of the Second World War that he held office. He then became Parliamentary Private Secretary to Oliver Lyttleton, president of the Board of Trade, in 1941, and in the Coalition Government that operated until May 1945, he was Joint Parliamentary Secretary at the Ministry of Supply. In the Caretaker Government of 1945, he was Parliamentary Secretary to the Ministry of National Insurance.

Alongside him in that Caretaker Government, which lasted just two months, was the Sixth Earl of Rosebery who, as Lord Dalmeny, had captained Surrey from 1905 to 1907.

Son of a Prime Minister and brother-in-law of Lord Aberdare, a most capable batsman, Lord Dalmeny was in the Eton XI in 1900 and played for Buckinghamshire while still at school. He appeared for Middlesex against Sussex and Essex at the end of July 1902, when it was apparent that he was a very useful middle-order batsman. In 1903, he first played for Surrey who were experiencing a period of drought after some years of success. There was a crisis of captaincy, and the side was rudderless. There was no settled XI, and, in 1904, no fewer than 40 players were used.

In an effort to halt the decline, the Surrey Committee asked John Raphael to lead the side in 1905 as soon as his term at Oxford was complete. Until Raphael became available Lord Dalmeny was asked if he would captain the side. His impact on Surrey cricket was immediate, proving to be a most energetic and capable captain. His fairness, humour and authority (although he was only 23) won him respect from all, and what had previously been a group of ill-disciplined individuals now became a team with zest and enthusiasm. A nucleus of 15 players replaced the former motley selections. Both spirits and performance soared.

So quick was the success that, with Raphael's whole-hearted approval and agreement, Dalmeny was asked to continue until the end of the season. In fact, he captained the county until 1907 season when pressure of business and politics forced him to stand down. He was Liberal Member for Midlothian from 1906 to 1910, so here was a working MP at the wicket.

It should not be imagined that Dalmeny was simply a titled gentleman whose social standing gave him a place in the side and automatically made him leader. He was a good cricketer. In his first season as captain, he hit centuries against Leicestershire and Warwickshire and reached 1,000 runs as he did in 1907, his last season.

He also used his considerable influence to Surrey's advantage off the field. In 1905, he approached the Club's Patron, the Prince of Wales, later King George V, for permission to use the Prince's feathers as the County's badge. It was granted. There was another event of which Lord Dalmeny was even more proud. It was he who first included Jack Hobbs in the Surrey side, and quickly gave him his county cap.

The last of Lord Dalmeny's 94 games for Surrey came in 1908. In those matches, he had hit 3386 runs. His first-class average of 22.47 and 50 catches shows a good cricketer. Inevitably, he served in the First World War with distinction, and his last first-class appearance was for MCC against Nottinghamshire at the beginning of the 1920 season. He finished unbeaten on 11 as his side won.

He never lost his interest in cricket, serving as president of Surrey from 1947 to 1949, and of MCC in 1953, but, after the death of his father in 1929 when he became the Sixth Earl of Rosebery, he was most celebrated in the world of horse racing as an owner of distinction and considerable success. This was evident from the fact that he left in excess of nine million pounds when he died in 1974 at the age of 92.

In his rich and varied life, Lord Rosebery's political activity was less active than one might have expected, and his involvement in government was restricted to those two months and a day as Secretary of State for Scotland in the Caretaker Administration of 1945.

Like Rosebery, Peat's place in government ended in 1945, but he remained active in accountancy, being president of the Institute of Chartered Accountants, 1959-60.

By one of those coincidences which have pervaded this narrative, the first of the three wickets that Peat took in the Varsity match of 1913 was that of the Hon Henry George Hill Mulholland, the Cambridge captain. Mulholland, second son of Baron Dunleath, had been in a strong Eton XI which included Lionel Tennyson, R. H. Twining and 'Buns' Cartwright and had won his blue in Ireland's side of 1911. An innings of 78 had been instrumental in bringing his side victory in 1912, and he led them to a four-wicket win in 1913.

Playing alongside Falcon in his first year in the Cambridge side, Mulholland had impressed with innings of 75 and 61 against Sussex, and 153 against the All India touring side which, at that time, was 19 years away from Test status. There were centuries against Northamptonshire in 1913 and against MCC in 1914 when he was again expected to play in the Varsity match, 'but in deference to high authority, the idea was abandoned. Though he had only played three times against Oxford, Mulholland had been in residence four years, and his appearance at Lord's would have involved an infringement of the agreement come to by the Universities nearly 50 years ago.' According to *Wisden*, he was sorely missed by Cambridge.

If Mulholland's defence was considered suspect, none faulted his attacking play. His off-drive had a hint of glory about it. In 32 first-class matches, he scored 1,642 runs, average 30.40, and took 51 wickets at 23.86 runs each. Then came the First World War.

Serving as a lieutenant from 1914 to 1919, he was awarded the Distinguished Service Order, and when peace returned he was destined for Ireland and a political career. He became MP for County Down in 1921. Within five years, he was Assistant Private Secretary to the

Ministry of Finance in Northern Ireland. In 1929, he was elected Member for the Ards Division, and from then until his retirement in 1945, he was Speaker of the Northern Ireland House of Commons.

Sworn in as a Privy Councillor (Northern Ireland) in 1930 and created First Baron Mulholland on his retirement, he was to become both H. M. Lieutenant for County Londonderry and a governor of the BBC (Northern Ireland). He lived until he was 82, and throughout maintained that his recreations were cricket, golf and shooting – in that order.

Whether or not he met Lindsay Everard when he was at Trinity College, Cambridge, we do not know. Certainly, the two were in residence at the same time, albeit for a short period. W. L. Everard had not played against Mulholland when he was at Harrow, and he was never close to winning a place in the XI at Cambridge. He was, like many of us, one of those whose enthusiasm outstripped his ability although it is probably true to say that his first love was flying.

A Leicestershire man by birth and residence, he spent the First World War in the Leicestershire Yeomanry and the First Life Guards. He had begun a long association with the Leicestershire Gentlemen's Club when he came down from university, and he was secretary of the club for 21 years.

In 1924, Leicestershire entered their 2nd XI in the Minor Counties Championship for the first time. The side 'met with a gratifying measure of success,' according to *Wisden*, 'sharing 11th place with Cheshire and the Lancashire 2nd XI.' For Everard, the season was memorable, since he topped the Leicestershire batting averages with 165 runs, average 33. He was well ahead of the second man, Les Berry, but it was Berry who got an extended run in the first team and graced the middle county with his presence for the next 25 years. Everard was given a place in the side which met Cambridge University at Leicester in mid-June, but the county was beaten. Everard made three and nought and never played first-class cricket again.

By the following season, he was no longer appearing in the 2nd XI, for business and politics had now absorbed him. In the same year that encompassed his first-class career, William Lindsay Everard had been elected MP for the Melton Division of Leicestershire. He was to hold the seat, as a Unionist, for the next 21 years. His contact with the county club remained, for he was president in 1936 and 1939 and a member of the MCC committee from 1938 to 1945.

He played his cricket for the Leicestershire Gentlemen and for Lords and Commons Cricket, but, as we have already indicated, he had a passion for flying. He had his own aerodrome near his home at Ratcliffe Hall where he pioneered private flying. His contribution to the development of flying was further marked when he was made Honorary Air Commodore, 605th County of Warwick Fighter Squadron, and knighted in 1939. He was ever a busy and energetic man but died at the age of 57 just four years after the end of his political career.

The flying craze was not restricted to Lindsay Everard. Harold Gilligan and Freddie Calthorpe, both of whom captained England in the period between the wars, were fliers, and Peter Thorp Eckersley shared Everard's passion to such an extent that he became known as the 'cricketer airman'.

The two men had much in common. Like Everard, Eckersley had won a place in his school side, Rugby, where he played alongside another future county captain, E. F. Longrigg of Somerset, but, also like Everard, he could find no place in the side at Cambridge. His home county – Lancashire – were more kind to him; he played for them against his university in June 1923, only to start his career with a 'duck'.

Eckersley appeared in four championship matches the following season, and, with Lancashire a growing power in the land, seven in 1925. *Wisden* claimed that he 'showed distinct improvement in batting, his 82 not out against Northamptonshire coming when failure might have meant the break-down of the side.' He confirmed that assessment in 1926 when, under Major Leonard Green, Lancashire won the championship for the first time in 22 years. Eckersley played in just under half of the county's championship matches and led the side on occasions. With Green suffering from an injured wrist, Eckersley captained Lancashire in the last, vital match of the season against Nottinghamshire.

To win the title Lancashire had to win and when Nottinghamshire were 234-4 at tea on the first day there seemed little chance they would do this. But Nottinghamshire were bowled out for 292, Makepeace hit a marvellous 180, and Lancashire won by ten wickets. There were scenes of great enthusiasm, with Eckersley and Arthur Carr, the Nottinghamshire captain, succeeding in rescuing the match ball which they autographed and presented to the Lancashire president.

The title was retained the following season when Eckersley played in 23 matches and hit 102 not out against Gloucestershire at Bristol. This was to be the only century of his career. He was prevented from playing at all in 1928, due to appendicitis, when Lancashire won the title under Green for the third year in succession.

Born in Newton-le-Willows, Eckersley was adopted as prospective Conservative and Unionist for his home constituency in 1928. The Westhoughton constituency had once been held by another Lancashire cricketer, Frank Hardcastle (1885-92), so Eckersley would be following a tradition, but he resigned his candidature and accepted the invitation to captain Lancashire instead. Frank Hardcastle, we should fleetingly note, played two matches only for Lancashire in 1868-69 as an amateur middle-order bat.

Back to Eckersley who Frank Thorogood, in *The Daily News*, suggested had tossed a coin to decide whether politics or cricket should be his career. Others said that Walter Brearley had persuaded him politics could wait. He certainly took on a most difficult task in succeeding Green, a most successful and popular captain, whilst still short of his 25th birthday.

Lancashire slipped to second in 1929, and the captain's batting showed a marked decline after his year's absence from the field. Limited as were his own abilities, Eckersley proved to be a good leader of men. He was well liked and he commanded respect, and if he lacked consistency at the crease, he was dynamic in the field. He was a man of wealth, and he had the time to give to a game that he loved. He was known as a merry-hearted skipper.

Against all expectations, he led Lancashire to their fourth title in five years in his second season in command. His side went through their championship programme undefeated, but three of the last five matches had to be won to clinch the title. The weather was not kind, and all depended on the last game, against Essex. Lancashire won with ease but in a rather dour manner. There were criticisms of the Red Rose style, particularly from Cardus who turned acidly against his county, but the main crime Lancashire committed was that of growing old and being too successful. *The Cricketer* saw the merry Eckersley as being in danger of becoming infected by those around him. Gustave Dore once painted a neophyte looking at the grizzly monks around him and obviously wondering if he would grow like them. So one can imagine Eckersley, a gallant hard-hitting run-getter, wondering whether in time he will adopt the cautious, careful characteristics of his companions.

Eckersley had enjoyed a revival with the bat and had captained the champions. Now he turned his attention again to politics. At the August General Election, 1931, the National Government was swept to office. Eckersley stood as the Conservative National candidate at Leigh. He polled 21,837 votes, but his Labour opponent – not on the National ticket – won 23,965 votes and took the seat. So Mr J. Tinker reversed the trend of the rest of the country. Peter Eckersley returned to the job of captaining Lancashire.

The great Lancashire side of the 20s was now breaking up, with Hallows, Makepeace, McDonald and Richard Tyldesley all departing, but Eckersley was captain of the champions again in 1934, once more to the surprise of many.

He was an immensely popular figure in the game, but he could sometimes excite criticism for his tactics. Jim Swanton remembered that Lancashire met Sussex at Eastbourne in the penultimate match of that 1934 season, when they concentrated solely on winning first innings points. Swanton criticised the attitude both in print and to Eckersley at dinner, but the Lancashire captain was unrepentant, insisting that the title meant money to his professionals and most likely an increase in winter pay. That overrode all other considerations. 'His side were as devoted to their captain as he was to them.'

He was not without eccentricities. He had a reputation for motor cars and aeroplanes, and he was known to fly to a county match. In 1935, he created cricket history when he hired a plane to take his side from Swansea to Southampton. The same year, he won the Exchange Division of Manchester as a Conservative and Unionist again supporting the National ticket. He resigned the captaincy of Lancashire, and never played for the county again.

Eckersley had a restless, energetic nature. He played for Lords and Commons, and he flew and he drove, and, in 1938, he appeared for An England XI against the Australians at Blackpool, his last first-class match. Eckersley led Lancashire through a transitional period, but won two championships in his seven years as captain, and brought into the side such men as Washbrook, Pollard, Phillipson and Paynter.

Not always in the best of health, but always full of energy, he joined the Air Arm of the Royal Naval Volunteer Reserve as soon as war broke out in 1939. In August 1940, he was killed in a flying accident at the base in Eastleigh, in Hampshire. It was a death of tragic irony, just a month past his 36th birthday. Few men pack so much into their lives.

Peter Thorp Eckersley played in 292 first-class matches, scored 5,629 runs (average 19.54), and held 121 catches. These are not figures that are likely to earn him a permanent place in the history of the game, but he is the only Member of Parliament ever to have captained a county that won the championship. That is likely to be a record he will never lose.

Nothing could more appropriately complete a chapter about 'Gentlemen and Eccentrics' in the inter war years than the assumption in 1929 by the 3rd Baron Tennyson of his place in the Upper House. Subsequently there is little political activity to note but in the cricketing sphere Lionel Tennyson's story is the stuff of legends.

Tennyson's cricket at Eton (where else?) centred on his fast bowling which then fell away to the extent of his not achieving an anticipated blue at Cambridge. He was, however, developing his batting – attacking as one might expect from a man of strong build and forceful character. He first appeared for Hampshire in 1913 after a century for the MCC v Oxford University on his first-class debut and subsequently played 347 matches for them until retirement, captaining the county with vigour from 1919-33.

Only a modest success in his first five Test matches – he was barely required on this triumphant tour of South Africa in 1913-14 – there was a pause for the First World War. Twice wounded and twice mentioned in despatches, Tennyson showed his Rifle Brigade courage yet again in 1921. Returning for the Lord's Test against Armstrong's all-conquering Australians, his second innings knock of 74 not out in a total of 283 encouraged a criticised set of selectors to make him captain for the next three Tests. At Leeds England lost again, despite Tennyson scoring a famous 63 batting at number 9 in effect with only one hand after an injury in the field. It took him only 80 minutes – those powerful forearms again – and he added a further 36 in the second innings, still injured.

The final two Tests were drawn, with a further 52 from the skipper at The Oval. Three fifties in five innings against those Australians puts his Test career record in a higher perspective than the figures alone: 31.36 in nine matches. But, one suspects, his greatest joy in that season would have been in collecting £50 for a bet that he would score at least one 50 at Lord's and winning a 1,000-1 wager rashly made by a friend in 1920 that he would never captain England.

Tennyson's subsequent career was as lively as the Test match episode. His Hampshire captaincy was never dull. When umpires objected to over-numerous vocal contacts with his batsmen at the crease, he sent instructions by telegram with the post office messenger boy carrying an envelope to the crease. Most of the captain's orders fell into the 'get on with it' category. He rarely needed such injunctions himself. One blow at Southampton covered 140 yards. Playing against Yorkshire at Lord's, he hit the pavilion roof four times in an innings.

His first-class career average of 23.33 (19 centuries) in 477 matches only gives a hint at the fun – which included several overseas tours to South Africa, Jamaica and even India as late in his cricketing life as 1937-38. There was a throwback to his Poet Laureate grandfather, a poem he wrote to mark Percy Chapman's successful Australian tour in 1928-29. A sum of £100 demanded by Tennyson as the only poem written by one England captain about another was not met, so he published it himself.

Sad, indeed, that the Third Baron Tennyson was rarely in the Upper House even in the later years before his death in 1951. One suspects he would have made it more lively outside the Chamber, if not within it. Ian Peebles records, 'When he entered a room, everyone smiled'.

Going In at
Number 10

WHEN the then Fourteenth Earl of Home accepted the Queen's invitation to form a Government on 20 October 1963, he was not only the first peer of the realm to become Prime Minister for more than 60 years, he was also the first ever first-class cricketer to do so.

Few cricketers have had such a varied, if brief, first-class career as Lord Dunglass, as he then was, and few men have had such a dazzling and varied political experience. Elected as Conservative Member for South Lanark in 1931, he held the seat for 14 years. He was Parliamentary Private Secretary to the Prime Minister, Neville Chamberlain, from 1937 until 1940, and, in the month-long Caretaker Government of 1945, he was Joint Parliamentary Under Secretary at the Foreign Office.

In 1950, he became Conservative MP for the Lanark Division of Lanarkshire, but a year later, he succeeded to the title of Lord Home. He was, successively, Minister of State, Scottish Office, and Secretary of State for Commonwealth Relations. By this time he was also Deputy Leader of the House of Lords. He was Leader of the House of Lords

1959-60 and Lord President of the Council. In July 1960, he was appointed Foreign Secretary in Harold Macmillan's Government.

Macmillan suffered considerable pressure and fatigue in the last three years of his Ministry. He had to survive the Profumo affair and the Denning Report, and he had worked tirelessly to bring about the Test Ban Treaty. Macmillan became concerned about his own state of health, and increasingly felt that he should not continue in office. Speculation grew as to who would, or should, succeed. Harold Wilson had taken over the Labour Party, and opposition now threatened more vigorously than they had done for many years. Butler, Maudling, Heath, Macleod and Hailsham were seen by Conservative MPs as the men most likely to succeed Macmillan.

Inevitably, after so long in office, Macmillan's power and popularity was waning, with the Conservative Party was losing ground in opinion polls. Having undergone an operation, Macmillan was unable to attend the Party Conference at Blackpool when Lord Home was the chairman. Rumour and public disputes were rife, and the conference was described as chaotic. Through a message read at the conference, Macmillan intimated that he was standing down.

Hailsham leapt too soon into the limelight to proclaim his candidature. Butler was the natural successor as the man who had done so much to help Macmillan to bring wealth and liberal conservative progress to the country, but he was not liked by all within the party. Lord Home suddenly emerged as the man who could blunt the power-seeking of some and be an acceptable alternative to others.

Home was approached with a view to becoming Leader of the Conservative Party. He went to see his doctor, and, in his own droll words, he reported that 'unfortunately said I was fit'. Lord Home duly became Leader of the Conservative Party and Prime Minister. He disclaimed his peerage for life on 23 October 1963, and the following month he became Sir Alec Douglas-Home, MP for Kinross and West Perthshire. He held the seat until his retirement 11 years later.

When he took over the leadership of the Conservative Party the standing of the Government was at a low ebb, but he effected a remarkable recovery which saw them lose only narrowly to Harold Wilson and the Labour Party in October 1964. Sir Alec Douglas-Home now became Leader of the Opposition for the next nine months. He then stepped down as Leader of the Conservative Party in favour of Edward Heath, and when Heath won the election in June 1970, became Foreign Secretary for a second time. After four years – not the easiest period in which to hold the post – he retired when the Labour Party was returned to power in March 1974. At the age of 71, he became Lord Home of the Hirsel.

The Homes were always a spirited family of varied accomplishments, none more so than Lord Home's younger brother, William Douglas-Home, the dramatist, who listed golf and politics as his recreations but also fought elections in Scotland first as a Progressive Independent and then as a Liberal. Perhaps the sparks of individuality in Lord Home, whose major qualities as a politician were his honesty, loyalty and trustworthiness, manifested themselves most in his cricket.

As Lord Dunglass, he won a place in the Eton XI in 1921 and was considered good enough to be recognised as an all-rounder. He opened the innings in the match against Harrow, at Lord's, and averaged 21.22 for the season. His bowling was used sparingly, but he took six wickets in 46 overs.

His young talents were more fully developed a year later. In reviewing the Public Schools' cricket of 1922, H. S. Altham was not too kind to Eton whose batting he generally considered dull. He found an exception in Lord Dunglass who was particularly adept on slow or damp wickets. 'He had the courage of his convictions and could hook and pull the turning ball effectively, as he proved in both of the school matches.'

Altham was full of praise, too, for the bowling of Lord Dunglass, who '…was not really discovered as a bowler until well on in the season, but on a wet wicket he was probably the most useful of the Etonians; he could keep a length and seemed often able to force some life out of an apparently dead pitch.'

In the meeting with Harrow at Lord's, the young all-rounder

excelled himself. The game was ruined by rain, and Eton's batting was considered tedious, but Lord Dunglass was the exception. In just over an hour, he and E. W. Dawson, a future Leicestershire and Cambridge University captain, added 103. Dunglass made 66 of them, hitting three fours and five threes on a slow outfield.

He followed his fine batting performance with bowling figures of 4-37 from 18 overs, the victims including the brilliant Leonard Crawley. His all-round cricket for Eton earned Dunglass a place in the Lord's Schools against the Rest. Having batted at number three for Eton, he found himself at number eight in the Schools' side, but then Duleepsinhji was at number seven. In a total of 105, Dunglass hit 14, and he had the best bowling figures for the Schools' side, 3-22.

Dunglass went up to Christ Church, Oxford, where many predicted a good cricket career for him at the university. He appeared in the Freshmen's match for C. H. Knott's XI, batted at number three, hitting 24 (second top score) and 6, and took the wickets of both openers in the first innings at a cost of 32 runs, but Oxford did not call upon his services in 1923.

Surprisingly, his first-class debut was to be against Oxford at the beginning of the following season. He appeared for Middlesex against the university, batted at number five and scored 1 and 3. He had match figures of 3-51, but still no call came to play for the Dark Blues. Indeed, his other first-class match that season was again against his own university. He played for the Free Foresters at the end of May, and, at number ten, was twice unbeaten, for 4 and 37. In the second innings, he and R. H. Bettington added 113 for the ninth wicket, the Foresters' best stand of the match. Dunglass was grossly underbowled but took the wicket of J. L. Guise for 30 runs.

His first-class cricket in 1925 was limited to Middlesex's opening fixture, once more versus Oxford University, when he hit 19 and took 1-30 in two innings. He did, of course, play in other matches during the season which did not have first-class status, most notably for Berwickshire and District against Kent when the southern county toured Scotland at the end of the season in England. It was a 12-a-side match, and 'Tich' Freeman totally bemused the Scotsmen in their second innings, taking 10-34 in 12 overs. One of his victims was Lord Dunglass, who was top-scorer with 21.

In 1926, he at last played for Oxford University. He led one of the sides in the Seniors' Trial Match, and he might have expected to play in the early fixtures. Sadly, the matches against Kent and Middlesex, scheduled to begin the season, were cancelled because of the General Strike. Lord Dunglass played in two of the 'out' matches. At Lord's, he captured the wicket of the great West Indian, George Challenor, in each innings when he bowled against MCC, and his other wicket in that match was that of the even greater 'Patsy' Hendren. At Chelmsford, against Essex, he bowled only 11 overs in the match. There was still to be no blue.

Earlier that season, he had again appeared against the university, returning the best bowling figures of his career, 3 and 43, for H. D. G. Levenson-Gower's XI. It is a measure of the strength of the Oxford side of this period that they could call upon nine old blues, but they were still beaten in the Varsity match by a Cambridge side which included E. W. Dawson (Dunglass' Old Etonian partner), Turnbull, Duleepsinhji, Enthoven, Robins and Meyer.

In the winter of 1926-27, Lord Dunglass went on tour to South America with an MCC side under the captaincy of Pelham Warner. It was a remarkably strong side for such a tour, including G. O. Allen, J. C. White, G. R. Jackson (the Derbyshire captain), Gerry Weigall and R. T. Stanyforth. There were four 'Test' matches against Argentina, and Dunglass played in three of these although the bowling at Warner's disposal was so formidable that he allowed Dunglass only one over in all.

Back at home, in 1927, Lord Dunglass played his tenth and last first-class match. It was for Harlequins against Oxford University, at Oxford. He scored four and took the wicket of R. H. Horsley.

Thereafter, the cricket of the future Prime Minister was of a more gentle nature. He played many times for Lords and Commons Cricket before and after the Second World War, and if the tear-away fast medium bowler had reduced his pace to somewhat slower off-cutters, he still batted with force and purpose. He was, of course, president of MCC in 1966, and of Lords and Commons Cricket in 1988 by which time honours had been heaped upon him from all over the country. We should, however, take a closer look at his first-class career.

He played ten matches, batted 15 times, hit 147 runs, and averaged 16.33. He made eight catches and took 12 wickets for 363 runs. It is not a mighty record, but it is not a bad one for a young amateur feeling his way, and even at this distance, one suspects he was deserving of more opportunities to prove himself. Anyone who could bowl 'Patsy' Hendren could not have been that bad a player.

The remarkable thing about Alec Douglas-Home's career is that in ten matches he represented six different sides – Middlesex, Oxford University, MCC, Free Foresters, Levenson-Gower's XI and Harlequins – and in five of his matches he appeared against the university where he was in residence. If Lord Home of the Hirsel's political career was long, rich and wide-ranging his first-class career in cricket was, if brief, no less varied and was touched with the exotic, even eccentric. He is the only Prime Minister to have played first-class cricket, but is he the best cricketer to have lived at Number 10 Downing Street or, indeed, the cricketer with the closest connections to the first-class game to have been the incumbent of that terraced house? Let us explore.

The Fifth Earl of Rosebery obviously has some claim in that his son, Lord Dalmeny, captained Surrey with great aplomb and twice hit 1,000 runs in a season. As we have said, with two first-class hundreds to his credit, Lord Dalmeny was a capable cricketer, but he became better known for his success as a race-horse owner. In this sport, he followed his father, but while the Sixth Earl gained renown in the 1930s for being a patron of the Turf, the involvement of the Fifth Earl in the same recreation was frowned upon at the end of last century. He had succeeded Gladstone, a man of moral rectitude, and Rosebery lost votes through his association with the Turf which, through betting, was seen as a threat to morality. It was also thought that a statesman who could afford time for such frivolous pursuits was not likely to be a worthy successor to the Grand Old Man.

In political terms, cricket has generally escaped being considered a frivolous pastime, and has often been the sport of prime ministers if not of Kings. Clement Attlee, who did not make the XI at Haileybury, predated Peter Brooke in being a walking encyclopaedia on the game. When he became Prime Minister in July 1945, he gave high priority to the tape machine which gave regular county scores, and he acquiesced in pairing so that Lords and Commons Cricket matches might go ahead untroubled. An avid cricket statistician, he is said to have once sacked a minister by telling him that he had had a good innings, but it was now time for him to return to the pavilion. Hopefully the victim took this sporting phrase with understanding.

Another Labour Prime Minister, Harold Wilson, was the first captain of cricket at Wirrall Grammar School, and a third, James Callaghan, was opposed in his Cardiff constituency by the captain of England, but neither Attlee, Wilson nor Callaghan can really challenge Lord Home's right to claim Number 10 as his spot.

The same must apply to Harold Macmillan whose grandson, Mark Faber, won a blue at Oxford and played for Sussex for four seasons. An elegant right-handed batsman, he hit three first-class centuries, Mark Faber died tragically young in 1991.

Stanley Baldwin's threat to Alec Douglas-Home for supremacy at Number 10 demands closer scrutiny.

Baldwin was an unexpected Prime Minister. Lord Curzon had called him 'a man of the utmost insignificance', but he was to prove all too significant in Curzon's life. Baldwin had been an important industrialist and only entered politics late in life. He became closely associated with Bonar Law at the Treasury and was, for a short time, Chancellor of the Exchequer. When Bonar Law was compelled to resign as Prime Minister through ill health in May 1923, Baldwin succeeded him although this decision had not been a foregone conclusion. Lord Curzon, the Foreign Secretary, had believed the election would light on him, and was bitterly disappointed that he was passed over, but King George V held the opinion that the days had gone when it was possible for a Prime Minister to be in the Lords.

Between May 1923 and May 1937, Stanley Baldwin was Prime Minister three times, and virtually ruled the country during that period. Through Stanley Jackson, as we have noted, he brought Winston Churchill back into the Conservative fold, and he also won praise for defeating The General Strike.

As the First Earl Baldwin of Bewdley, he was president of MCC in 1938, for he did not regard cricketers, as did his relation, as flannelled fools. Far from it. If no great player, he was an enthusiast. When Captain John Isaac was killed in action in 1915 Baldwin managed the affairs of his estate for his widow. Isaac, a gentleman jockey who had ridden the winner of the Cairo Grand National in 1911, was a friend who had played for Worcestershire in Edwardian times.

Some years after this, in 1934, Baldwin's daughter, Mrs Richard Munro, married for a second time. Her husband was George Kemp-Welch who had come down from Cambridge where he had won his blue for soccer and for three years for cricket, captaining the side in 1931. He was remarkably successful against Oxford, averaging 45 in his three appearances. An attractive opening batsman, he and E. T. Killick began Cambridge's innings with a partnership of 139 in 1930, and the following year, he and Ratcliffe shared an opening stand of 149.

Kemp-Welch was also a very useful fast medium pace bowler, and he was chosen for the Gentlemen and for the Rest of England. In the summer vacations, he appeared regularly for Warwickshire, and had he been more often available, he would have made a mark in county cricket. Brother of the well known diarist, Betty Kenwood, Kemp-Welch toured Jamaica twice with Lord Tennyson's team, hitting 186 against All Jamaica in 1932.

To the chagrin of his father-in-law, Kemp-Welch played no more first-class cricket after 1936 when he was 29. To the sadness of all, he was killed in 1944 when a bomb dropped on the Guards Chapel in Chelsea. He had joined the Grenadier Guards at the outbreak of war and had risen to the rank of captain. A brilliant fielder, as befitted a man who had played centre-forward and captained Cambridge, he was much missed.

Proud as he was of his son-in-law, Stanley Baldwin was even prouder of his wife. In 1892, he married Lucy, elder daughter of Edward Lucas Jenks Ridsdale of Rottingdean. She shared Baldwin's faith and was a perfect partner, prompting him with an undying energy and a quality of speech that matched his own. She was, in every respect, the power behind the throne of the Prime Minister.

In the mid-1930s, the Western Brothers – sardonic, school-tie humorists at the piano who pleaded with cads to play the game – sung about Mrs Baldwin's funny little hats. They little knew that they were singing not just about the Prime Minister's wife, but about an outstanding cricketer.

In the last quarter of the 19th century, cricket for women flourished in the great country houses, and, in 1887, the first club, White Heather, was formed. Its score-book relates that it came into being owing to 'the large amount of cricket being played at Normanhurst and Eridge', the country seats of the Brassey and Neville families. White Heather was founded in Nun Appleton, Yorkshire, by eight ladies who were either of aristocratic birth or independent means. They adopted the name from their favourite badge, and the colours of pink, white and green for the same reason.

The club's most celebrated player was Lucy Ridsdale whose father was a high ranking officer at the Royal Mint responsible for determining the amount of gold or silver in coins. Legend has it that Stanley Baldwin saw Lucy Ridsdale playing cricket and fell in love with her immediately. This is most likely for, in 1892, the year of their marriage, the future Mrs Baldwin averaged 62 with the bat. When one considers that the leading batsman of the year, Arthur Shrewsbury, averaged under 42 in the County Championship, Lucy Ridsdale's achievement was remarkable.

One would also dare to suggest that the finest cricketer to have inhabited Number 10 Downing Street was not Lord Home of the Hirsel, but Mrs Stanley Baldwin, née Lucy Ridsdale of the White Heather Club.

Last Men In

HON ROBERT John Remnant succeeded to the title of Second Baron Remnant in 1933 after which he scored heavily in Lords and Commons Cricket, particularly against MCC He hit 116 against them in 1939. He played his county cricket for Berkshire, and represented the Minor Counties three times in first-class matches between 1931 and 1936, averaging 28.50 and taking five wickets with his medium pace. The record of his younger brother, Peter Farquharson, is more interesting.

Peter Remnant was educated at Eton and Magdalen College, Oxford, but he did not reach the school XI or win his blue. In 1916, at the age of 19, he was serving as a lieutenant in the army. From 1920 to 1938, he played with distinction for Berkshire. In 1929, he did not enjoy the best of seasons but was selected for the Minor Counties' side to play the visiting South Africans at Stoke-on-Trent.

The match was significant for the fact that, at the age of 54, the great S. F. Barnes bowled unchanged throughout the first South African innings to take 8-41 in 32 overs. This tended to overshadow Peter Remnant's performance. He opened the innings with Cook, captain of the Surrey 2nd XI, and the pair scored 102 in under an hour against a strong attack. Remnant hit 62, the highest score of the innings, but when he batted a second time he was run out for 0. He did not appear in first-class cricket again although, as we have stated, he played for Berkshire until 1938.

He served with the Royal Artillery throughout the Second World War, first in anti-aircraft battalions and then, as a Lieutenant-Colonel, on the staff. Tragically, his only son was killed in action early in 1945. In 1950, he was elected Conservative MP for the Wokingham Division of Berkshire. He stood down in 1959, but during his nine years in Parliament played occasionally for Lords and Commons Cricket.

Peter Remnant is one of many Parliamentarians whose first-class careers have been restricted to one match, but of all these single-game players, perhaps the most noteworthy is Sir Walter Turner Monckton.

The eldest son of a paper manufacturer, Walter Monckton went to Harrow where he developed the most ardent of passions for cricket. So great was his love of the game that he worked assiduously to make himself a good wicketkeeper worthy of a place in the XI despite the fact that he could hardly see out of one eye.

He played in the renowned Fowler's Match of 1910. This was the game in which Harrow, having led by 165 runs on the first innings, were bowled out for 45 in their second when they needed only 55 to win. The tormentor was an off-spinner named Fowler who took 8-23. Monckton, who had made 20 in the first innings, was bowled by Fowler for 0.

Monckton pulled off one stumping in the match, and the bowler to prosper was his friend, Harold Alexander, who, 45 years later, as Earl Alexander of Tunis, was to become president of MCC in the year before Monckton was to enjoy that same honour.

In 1910, Walter Monckton won an exhibition to Hertford College, but he went instead as a commoner to Balliol. Playing on R. H. Twining's side in the Freshmen's Match, he hit 27 and 33, held two catches and made a stumping, but he won no place in the Oxford side, nor did he after, playing without success in the Seniors' Match in 1913.

It was in his first season at Oxford, 1911, that he made his one first-class appearance. A combined Oxford and Cambridge side met a combined Army and Navy side at Portsmouth. Monckton scored 29 and 43, held a catch and took a stumping. As he was not out in his first innings, batting at number 11, he has the highly respectable batting average in first-class cricket of 72.

Among a brilliant set of undergraduates at Balliol, he took a third in Classical Honour Moderations in 1912, and a second in History in 1914. In 1913, he was president of the Union, and he met and became friendly with Edward, Prince of Wales, who was then at Magdalen. Their lives were later to draw even closer.

He played cricket and he hunted, but his near blindness in one eye prevented him from joining the army. Frustrated, he took preliminary examinations for the Bar, but he refused to give in to his disability. Aided by a younger brother, he obtained a commission in the army, served in France and was awarded the Military Cross.

In 1919, he was called to the Bar and enjoyed a varied and flourishing practice at common law. He was Recorder at Hythe, 1930 to 1937, and Chancellor to the diocese of Southwell for much of the same period. More significantly, he became Attorney General to the Prince of Wales in 1932.

He was a constitutional adviser in Hyderabad and Bhopal as India was moving towards federalism, and he visited India often. He was recalled abruptly when the crisis over King Edward VIII's relationship with Mrs Simpson began to develop and was deeply involved in the events which led up to the abdication. As the King's closest friend and confidant, he was often his sole companion, and when Edward drove to Portsmouth on the night of 11 December 1936, Monckton accompanied him. He was knighted a few weeks later, and, until the outbreak of war, he acted as a liaison between King George VI and the now Duke of Windsor.

In 1939, Sir Walter was appointed chairman of the Aliens Advisory Committee, but, ever active, he applied to join the RAFVR. Instead, he was made Director General of the Press and Censorship Bureau. Working for the Ministry of Information, he travelled to Russia, to Cairo, to the United States, Canada and Sweden. There were differences of opinion with Churchill which put him out of favour, but throughout the war he was always engaged in government tasks.

He had taken no active part in politics since his days at Oxford, and, in many ways was a-political, but, for that two months in 1945, he was Solicitor General in the Caretaker Government.

Monckton led the UK delegation on Reparations to Moscow and Potsdam, but when Labour came to power in July 1945, he returned to his practice at the Bar. He had an insatiable appetite for work and was active in public inquiries and Parliamentary committees.

He numbered Stafford Cripps among his close friends, and, in January 1946, went to India to help define the future of the princely states in an independent country. He worked furiously and successfully, but his efforts were sabotaged by extremists. The Indian Army settled further argument or debate.

In February 1951, to his great surprise, he was asked by Churchill to fight Bristol West in the by-election caused by the death of Oliver Stanley. Two days after his election, he was appointed Minister of Labour and National Service. He hesitated to accept the post, protesting to Churchill that he had no qualifications for the job. Churchill replied that he had the one qualification necessary, no political past.

Monckton was a success in the post. An unpretentious man of great charm, he established a warm relationship with the unions, and, in a time of strife and strikes, the two sides had a mutual respect for each other.

In 1955, he moved to defence and found himself at the heart of an international crisis. He was opposed to the Egyptian nationalisation of the Suez Canal in 1956, but equally hostile to the military intervention which the Government adopted. He became Paymaster General, and a year later, he retired from politics. Sympathetic and warm, he returned also to his first and greatest love, cricket, having two spells as president of Surrey as well as holding that senior post with MCC.

Created Viscount Monckton of Brenchley when he retired from politics, he never retired from life, and he must have been close to exhaustion when he died in 1965.

By chance, his son-in-law, Sir William Basil Goulding, a fine all-round sportsman, was also a wicketkeeper. He won a blue at Oxford for soccer, but not for cricket, and his only first-class match was for the Gentlemen of Ireland against MCC in 1934 when he scored 0 and 0 not out and did not claim a victim. His father-in-law had done better than that, and no man worked harder for his place in *Wisden* than Walter Monckton, nor overcome greater difficulties.

A contemporary of Remnant and Monckton in the Commons was Brigadier John Smyth who, having fought a Wandsworth seat in 1945, was elected as Conservative Member for Norwood in 1950.

Born in 1893, Smyth was a soldier of repute. Repton and Sandhurst led to the First World War where he won the Victoria Cross in 1915. Later he raised the 19th ('Dagger') Division which was famous for its part in Second World War successes at Mandalay and Rangoon. Indeed it was in India, playing for the Europeans in 1922-23, that he wins entry to these pages but the actual record is unknown to us. Better recognised is Jackie Smyth's Parliamentary career in the Ministry of Pensions and National Insurance 1951-55. He was also an author, lecturer, and playwright, especially after leaving the Commons in 1966.

Jackie Smyth never hid his love of the game, nor his involvement in it. Lord Silkin of Dulwich was, perhaps, more reticent about his playing days. A lower-order right-handed batsman and a leg-break and googly bowler, he captained the XI at Dulwich in 1936. He enjoyed a good season, topping the batting averages, and taking 36 wickets to dominate the bowling with A. C. Shirreff.

He went up to Trinity Hall, Cambridge, in 1937, took 4-43 in the Freshmen's Match but was not invited to play in another game. The following season, he played in another trial, for the Perambulators against the Etceteras, hitting 56. On the strength of this, perhaps, he made his first-class debut for the university against the Army. He scored two, took a catch and captured the wicket of G. A. Rimbault at a personal cost of 59 runs.

A fortnight later, he played for his native county, Glamorgan, against his university. He scored 2 and 0 and took the wicket of J. R. Thompson. Sam Silkin was a very good friend of the brother of Maurice Turnbull, the Glamorgan captain, and, knowing of Silkin's ambition to win a place in the side at Cambridge, Turnbull gave him the opportunity to prove himself against his university. Alas, he failed to impress as we have recorded, and Sam Silkin now concentrated on the academic life.

He took a first-class honours in the first two parts of the Law Tripos and was called to the Bar in 1941 by which time he was in the Royal Artillery, rising to the rank of Lieutenant-Colonel.

In 1964, he was elected to Parliament as Labour Member of Camberwell (Dulwich), but ten years later he became MP for Southwark (Dulwich). In all, Sam Silkin was a Member of Parliament for 19 years.

He was a member of the Royal Commission on the Penal System for England and Wales, 1965 to 1966, and chairman of the Parliamentary Labour Party's Group on Common Market and European Affairs, 1966 to 1970.

From 1970 to 1974, he was the Opposition's Front Bench Spokesman on Legal Matters, and when Labour came to office in March 1974, was duly appointed Attorney General, a post he held throughout the five years of that administration. He is, therefore, the last man to have had experience of first-class cricket and hold government office. Created a Life Peer in 1985, he had left his cricket long in the past.

There was, however, always someone at Westminster on the other side of the House who could remind Sam Silkin of those days at Cambridge and of his cricketing aspirations. He was another Welshman, although born in Hong Kong where his father was Chief Justice. His name was William Rupert Rees-Davies.

William Rees-Davies won a place in the Eton XI in 1935, and the following season he was the outstanding fast bowler in schools cricket, one of the very best since G. O. Allen. In the words of *Wisden*, he bowled well at the beginning of the season and magnificently at the end. Against Harrow, he took 5-66 and 3-47, and threatened to rout Harrow in the first innings, reducing them to 134-7 at lunchtime, but losing his length after the break.

For Lord's Schools against the Rest, he troubled all batsmen with his pace to take 6-67 and 1-41. He won a place in the Public Schools XI to play the Army, and, 'bowling in devastating fashion and taking five wickets for fewer than seven runs apiece', he helped the schools' side outplay their opponents on the first day. Alas, J. W. A. Stephenson of Essex hit a century on the second, and the Army won by 61 runs. Nevertheless, Rees-Davies finished with figures of 5-34 and 3-74, and great things were predicted for him. The young man who won the Victor Ludorum at Eton was seen as an England fast bowler of the future.

He went up to Trinity College, Cambridge, with expectations which were, perhaps, too high, and the burdens on a young man of 19 were too great. All began well. He was selected for the opening match against Sussex, bowled very fast, took three wickets in three overs, but then he repeatedly overstepped the mark and came in for heavy punishment.

Against Warwickshire, in the second match of the season, he took 4-21, the best performance of his career, as the county side were bowled out for 43. This was not to be the basis for better things. As *Wisden* commented: 'In an effort to work up extreme pace his long run sometimes took him over the crease and generally he was erratic.'

He played in seven matches, took 16 wickets at 30.81 runs each, and he did not win the blue which everyone had thought was certain to be his. In fairness, it must be said that no Freshman was included in the Cambridge side for the Varsity match in 1936. When one looks at the team that Cambridge fielded under Hugh Bartlett one can only reflect in wonder, for, among others, Bartlett had at his disposal Norman Yardley, Wilf Wooller, R. P. Nelson (the future Northamptonshire captain), Jahangir Khan (the Indian Test cricketer), Paul Gibb, 'Billy' Griffith, M. St J. Packe (a future Leicestershire captain), A. F. T. White (who was to lead Worcestershire after the war), P. M. Studd (Lord Mayor of London in 1970), and J. H. Cameron (the West Indian Test cricketer). It was a formidable array.

The team was not quite so strong in 1937, but Rees-Davies did not play in a single match, and the great fast bowling hope was forgotten. Suddenly, he reappeared in the Seniors' Match at the start of the 1938 season and bowled well enough to win a place in the side to meet Yorkshire. The Cambridge XI was now far weaker than it had been two years earlier, particularly in bowling. Rees-Davies was selected for eight matches – one against the Australian tourists, and he played in the Varsity match at Lord's. Some considered him rather lucky to get his blue, but Cambridge had conceded a series of huge totals, and the attack was one of the weakest for years.

Cambridge had the better of the draw in the Varsity match. Rees-Davies, with a run greatly reduced from his Eton days, was troubled by a strained side, and he was desperately unlucky to have two chances put down off his bowling. He finished with a single wicket.

The 22-year-old who, only three years earlier, had been seen as a prime candidate to open the England bowling and to cause devastation with his pace, now slipped quietly from the first-class scene with 15 first-class games behind him, in which he took 33 wickets at 43 runs apiece. He took Honours in History and Law, and was called to the Bar of the Inner Temple in 1939.

Commissioned in the Welsh Guards, he served in the Second World War but lost an arm in 1943, which ended any hope of a revival of his cricket career. Although he never complained of it, his wounds caused him considerable pain for the rest of his life.

His father had been the Liberal MP for Pembroke, but in 1950 and 1951, he contested South Nottinghamshire as a Conservative. He won the Isle of Thanet seat at a by-election in March 1953, and in 1974, Thanet West, which he held until his retirement in 1983.

He was on the Select Committee for Health and Social Services, and chairman of the Conservative Committee on Tourism, but he never hid his love of collecting pictures and antiques, and of racing. In relation to the last, he regularly proposed measures in the House of Commons regarding the liberalisation of gambling. As was noted in his obituary when he died in 1992, this led to him being nicknamed 'with varying degrees of affection, as the one-armed bandit'.

A year after the death of William Rees-Davies came the death of Aidan Crawley at the age of 85 so bringing the group of living Commons cricketers to extinction. Aidan Crawley must rank alongside F. S. Jackson, Alfred Lyttelton and William Ward as the best of parliamentary cricketers. The story of his life reads like the plot of a John Buchan novel.

The son of a churchman, Aidan Crawley was of a cricketing family. His father, Canon Arthur Crawley, played for MCC in 1897 and 1898. He had two uncles who played for Cambridge, a brother who played for Hampshire and Middlesex, and two cousins who played for Worcestershire and Essex, one of them – Leonard – a cricketer of outstanding ability. Since then, of course, a younger relative, John, has played for Lancashire and England. The Crawleys could, and did, field their own XI. As already mentioned, Aidan played for the Crawley XI against the Bridgeman XI when he was eight, and he led a Crawley XI against Lords and Commons in 1965.

Aidan Crawley was first in the Harrow side in 1924 at the age of 16 when K. E. Crawley was captain of the XI. The following year he played in the Public Schools' trial at Lord's, and, in 1926, he appeared in the match against the Army.

He went up to Trinity College, Oxford, and won his blue for cricket in each one of his four years at the university. Crawley scarcely did himself justice in the Varsity matches, but his record for the university marks him as one of the four finest batsmen ever to have played for Oxford. He hit nine centuries during his period of residence. Five of these centuries came in 1928 when he established an Oxford record with 1,137 runs in the season. It was in this year that he also hit 53 for the Gentlemen against the Players at Lord's, reaching his 50 by striking the great 'Tich' Freeman over what are now the Compton and Edrich Stands into the Nursery Ground for six.

He was a batsman of grace and style as well as remarkable power. There was always panache in his batting even if, as some critics would suggest, his natural ability was not matched by his temperament.

That his ability was natural is evidenced by the story he told in his autobiography *Look Before Your Leap* of his double century against Northamptonshire in 1929. He and his friend Alan Barber, the Oxford skipper who captained Yorkshire in 1930, went to a ball at Magdalen College, and, without going to bed, then drove in his snub-nosed Morris straight to Wellingborough where they were to play against Northamptonshire. They managed to get an hour of sleep when the start was delayed, but at 2.40pm went out to open the innings together. After half an hour of playing and missing, Crawley suggested to Barber that the only thing they could do was to 'have a go'. Barber got out, but at the end of the day, Crawley had hit 204 out of 287 in three and a quarter hours. He hit ten sixes and 22 fours. This innings resulted in Crawley's selection in the 12 for the coming Lord's Test against South Africa. On the morning of the match, the selectors were divided on whether to play Tom Killick or Aidan Crawley, and narrowly plumbed for Killick, who they did not appreciate was unwell. He made 0 and 1 in the match, with Crawley 12th man. It was as close to winning a Test cap as one could get.

He had begun to assist Kent, the county of his birth, during his first year at Oxford, but in 19 years, he played only 33 matches for them. He made two centuries for Kent, the higher of them being his 175 out of 257, with two sixes and 26 fours. This innings was against Essex at Southend, in August 1930, the match in which fast bowler Ken Farnes first played for Essex. The home side led by 23 on the first innings, but Farnes related later what then happened.

'This time Kent set about us, and before lunch Aidan Crawley had reached his century in 80 minutes. His driving was magnificent, and he punished all the bowlers alike.' One of the many outfielders was Aidan's cousin, Leonard Crawley – no mean golfer. According to legend he waved with pleasure as the two sixes vanished over his head.

'Tich' Freeman who had taken all ten Essex wickets in the first innings, took six more in the second, and Kent won by 277 runs. Farnes, brimming with the joy of youth at playing county cricket, was still in a state of bewilderment some nine years later when he wrote: 'I was shocked and incredulous when Aidan Crawley, after making 176 against us in Kent's second innings, told me that he was not going to play much more first-class cricket, as he was going to be too busy and didn't like the game anyhow.' That was an inaccurate remark. Crawley himself has written about his decision: 'I loved cricket and continued to play for village clubs and Lords and Commons until I was over 70, but I always regarded it as a game…There were so many other things one wanted to do.'

A trip to India with his friend Esmond Harmsworth, son of Lord Rothermere, diverted him from going to North Borneo for Unilever to a job on the *Daily Mail*. Almost immediately, he covered the crash of the airship R101 in France. In contrast, he was hunting correspondent for the paper, and in 1932, he gained a lobby ticket for the House of Commons. Reporting for the *Swansea Evening Post* and witnessing the social degradations of the 1930s led him more and more towards socialism.

By 1936, Crawley was becoming disillusioned with his work on the *Daily Mail*, being totally opposed to Lord Rothermere's policy of appeasement to the fascist dictators in Europe and the Far East. He resigned from the newspaper to move into documentary film-making. All his life he was to be a great resigner on points of principle.

With the backing of Archbishop Cosmo Lang, Crawley completed a successful series of films for schools on the Holy Land and the Middle East. He was script-writer, cameraman, producer and editor. At the same time, he joined the Labour Party, did commentaries for Movietone News and for the infant outside broadcast department of BBC Television. Uneasy about the international situation, he also joined the Auxiliary Air Force and qualified as a pilot.

Joining the RAF at the outbreak of war, he became frustrated as a fighter pilot whose only task, it seemed, was to fly night patrols over the English Channel. More to his liking was to be sent to Ankara, Turkey, in April 1940, as assistant air attache. In reality, he was a member of the Balkan Intelligence Service. He also operated in Yugoslavia and Bulgaria from which he escaped shortly before the Germans entered in March 1941.

He became a fighter pilot with 73 Squadron in Egypt, and, in July 1941, was shot down over the Western Desert. Taken prisoner and sent to a camp some 150 miles from Warsaw, he escaped and boarded a train from from Munich to Switzerland before being recaptured. Others to escape with him were Robert Kee, later to become a broadcaster, and Anthony Barber, a future Tory Chancellor.

Crawley subsequently escaped on several other occasions, but each time was recaptured. He was repatriated just in time to fight and win the Buckingham Division of North Buckinghamshire for Labour at the General Election in 1945. He was Parliamentary Private Secretary to successive Secretaries of State for the Colonies, but then held office from 1950 to 1951 as Parliamentary Under Secretary of State for Air.

Cricket also re-emerged after the war years. Crawley turned out for Kent against Nottinghamshire in 1947 and scored 44 and 8, adding 113 with Les Ames for the second wicket in the first innings. His final first-class match was for Free Foresters against his old university in May 1949, when he scored 19 and 7, opening the innings as ever. Thus his record in the first-class game stands 5,061 runs in 141 innings with 11 centuries and an average of 37.48.

He had, in 1948, played for Buckinghamshire, but something of the old magic was gone. For Lords and Commons whom he had played a major part in resuscitating after the war, he remained a heavy scorer, hitting a 50 for them as late as 1968 when he was 60 years old.

In 1951, when there was a swing against Labour he lost his Buckinghamshire seat by 54 votes, and returned to documentary film-making, this time for BBC Television for whom he presented a programme on current affairs, *Viewfinder*. In 1955, he was appointed editor and chief executive of the newly established ITN and, although he was there only a brief time, he made a massive contribution to television news coverage, introducing new faces like Chris Chataway, Robin Day and, later, Reggie Bosanquet. He forwarded the cause of women in television journalism and administration, but once more he was to resign on a matter of principle, refusing to accept cuts in budget and time allotted on television to news coverage.

This was not his last resignation for in 1957 he left the Labour Party on the issue of nationalisation. He worked with Sir Walter Monckton on the commission investigating the future of Rhodesia and Nyasaland, and he was also back again at the BBC. In a by-election in 1962, he narrowly won West Derbyshire for the Conservatives.

When he took his seat in the House of Commons he was booed by his former Labour colleagues. Certainly some of the measures he advocated regarding unions and strikes suggested that he had moved very much to the right. Nevertheless, he always maintained that a healthy opposition and a strong trade union movement was of major importance in a democracy.

Crawley won no promotion under Macmillan, and he left Parliament in 1967 to concentrate on his work with London Weekend Television. He wrote his autobiography and a biography of De Gaulle, and, amid a tragic domestic life, he maintained his interest in cricket. His wife, Virginia Cowles, a distinguished American war and foreign correspondent, was killed in a car crash in Spain in 1983 when Crawley himself was injured. Their two sons were killed in an air crash in Italy five years later.

Aidan Crawley was president of MCC in 1972, and the first chairman of the National Cricket Association, 1968 to 1975. In 1971, in collaboration with *The Cricketer*, he was an instigator of the National Village Championship. In effect, his best and most able work for the game was below the first-class level.

He was not without his eccentricities. Lieutenant-Colonel John Stephenson, one of the kindest and best of MCC secretaries, tells how a few years before Crawley's death he was invited to Paul Getty's box at Lord's. When Stephenson looked in for a few moments he found that Crawley was complaining that he had experienced problems getting into the ground. It seems that he had not brought his MCC membership card, but he had a press pass which the gatemen queried. When Stephenson inspected the pass he found that it was 30 years out of date.

If there has been a decline in the numbers of first-class players from the Commons, emergence of the new category of Life Peers in 1958 has revived the species in the Upper House.

The first such cricketing creation in 1969 was one of the most appropriate and charismatic figures to appear in these pages – Learie Constantine, Lord Constantine of Maravel and Nelson. He came from a cricketing family in Trinidad, his father Lebrun touring England with the first two West Indian teams of 1900 and 1906, scoring their first century (stumped Reynolds bowled Grace) at Lord's. An uncle on his mother's side, Victor Passall, also played for the West Indies. She, too, was a formidably frank lady. When the young Learie limped home after a blow to his leg, she gave him scant sympathy: "He who lives by the sword, dies by the sword."

Learie played with his father for Trinidad in 1922 and the next year himself toured England with the third West Indian team. His brilliant fielding was noted, first in the covers but subsequently also close in. Throughout his career, indeed, it is his fielding which places Constantine in the highest cricketing levels but he was also a dangerous, if often unorthodox hitter, and a skilful fast (later medium pace) bowler.

The comparison with Gilbert Jessop is inescapable. Both could be match winners whose value should not be judged by figures alone. A famous example is his performance against Middlesex at Lord's in 1928. He scored a face-saving 86 in 30 minutes in the first innings, then took 7 wickets for 57, and finally hit 103 out of 133 in an hour to give his side victory.

On the 1928 tour Constantine achieved the double (1,381 runs and 107 wickets, with 33 catches to boot) but failed in the three Tests. It was, however, enough to attract the attention of Nelson in the Lancashire League. The Australian Ted McDonald had been an earlier famous professional with them but when in 1929 they engaged Learie for a £750 fee, it made front page news. He played with them for nine seasons, earning £1,000 a year when cotton workers were typically at £100. It was seen as a successful decision. Nelson won the league title seven times during Connie's stay with them.

League cricket restricted Constantine's Test appearances over these years. Occasional vital contributions were made but his next (and final) full tour was around England in 1939, when he headed the bowling (103 wickets at 17.77). In his last Test at The Oval he scored a typically dramatic 79 and took 5-75 in the first England innings. His last first-class cricket was in 1945, captaining a Dominion team to victory at Lord's.

Although the first-class and test career averages are only modest, they do not reflect the impact Constantine so often made as a player. For the record they are 635 runs in his 18 Tests (average 19.24) with 58 wickets (30.10) and 28 catches. The first-class tally was 4,451 runs (24.32) 439 wickets (20.25) and 133 catches – but a second remarkable career was to follow.

During his time in Lancashire, Constantine had been active as a social worker and public speaker, studying law in his spare time. After successfully qualifying as a barrister, he returned to Trinidad to become an MP and Minister of Works. Back again to Britain, as his country's High Commissioner (1962-64), his speeches from major occasions to typical club cricket pavilion dinners were frequently as magnetic as his performances in the field.

Sadly Learie Constantine's time as a peer was brief – two years only in the Lords before he died in 1971. Even in that short span his contributions were memorable – as, indeed, was the man himself in a generous and exciting life.

For years thereafter, Lord Williams of Elvel remained the sole keeper of the cricketing flame in a Parliament which had seen some 50 first-class cricketers before him.

Deputy Leader of the Opposition in the House of Lords, spokesman on Environment and Defence, and on trade, industry, energy and much else, Charles Cuthbert Powell Williams is a Welshman who was born in Oxford and played for Essex. At Westminster School, he had a brilliant record as a cricketer. A forceful middle-order batsman, he averaged 86.25 in 1950, and 74.55 the following season when he was captain and represented the Public Schools against the Combined Services at Lord's.

Going up to Christ Church, Oxford, full of hope and energy, he failed to win his blue as a Freshman in spite of innings of 53 and 74 in two matches against Sussex. He forced his way into the side the next year, 1953, when he hit a maiden first-class century, 115 against Free Foresters, and did well in the Varsity match in which Oxford were narrowly beaten by a century from Dennis Silk.

Given his blue by Colin Cowdrey the following year, Charles Williams hit centuries against Lancashire and Hampshire and scored 774 runs for the university. Moreover, he played nine matches for Essex in the long vacation, bringing his total of runs to 1128, average 30.48. Of the university batsmen, only M. J. K. Smith stood above him. For Essex, this was a time of struggle, and the arrival of Williams was seen as a blessing.

In 1955, when he captained Oxford, his total number of runs and his average both improved, and he hit what turned out to be his only century for Essex. It came in the match at Leicester when Williams hit 119 and shared a fourth wicket stand of 200 in three hours with Doug Insole. Essex led by 61 runs on the first innings but lost the match by 59 runs.

If this form gave Essex great encouragement, the county was to be bitterly disappointed as further study and business kept Charles Williams away from the cricket field. He was to play in only 18 more matches for Essex over the next four seasons, and by the last of them, against Gloucestershire, at Leyton, in August 1959, it was apparent that lack of practice at the top level was beginning to take its toll. Essex had lost a fine batsman who scored more than 4,000 runs at an average of 38.20 in an all too brief career. He was also a very fine fielder with 60 catches in his 87 first-class matches.

With BP, the Bank of London and Montreal, and Eurofinance SA, his work took him to Rome, Brussels, Guatemala, the United States and Paris, but wherever he went he found time to play a game or two for the local British club.

In 1964, he stood as Labour Candidate in the Conservative stronghold at Colchester. He was unsuccessful, but he fought well, and his political commitment has never wavered.

He was a founder member of the Labour Economic Finance and

Taxation Association, and from 1971 to 1977, he was Managing Director of Baring Brothers, the Merchant Bankers. He then became chairman of the Government Prices Commission, but when his position was dissolved by Mrs Thatcher in 1979 he returned to banking with Henry Ansbacher and Co.

Awarded the CBE in 1980 and created a life peer in 1985, Charles Williams continues to fight on behalf of the good things in life. He is president of the Council for the Protection of Rural Wales and was for some time the chairman of that finest of recording orchestras, the Academy of St Martin in the Fields.

Music, real tennis and cricket are his abiding recreations. He protests that his appearance for the Lords against the Commons at The Oval in 1993 is to be his last cricket match. Certainly he has since contributed substantially to the literature of the game with his well received book on Sir Donald Bradman, placing 'the Don' skillfully within his social as well as cricketing setting.

Of Williams' last Varsity match, Hubert Doggart wrote: 'Oxford needed 313 to win in four and a quarter hours, and while M. J. K. Smith and C. C. P. Williams were together in a cultured fourth-wicket partnership of 103 in 90 minutes, victory was a possibility. Once Smith was caught at long-on, the game swung in Cambridge's favour. Like Leonidas against the Persians, however, the Oxford captain barred the way.'

But of all the words written about his cricket, Charles Williams relishes most a comment by E. W. Swanton. Writing of a partnership with Colin Cowdrey, Swanton said it had been impossible to distinguish one from the other at the crease.

Praise indeed, and a suitable introduction to the first of two final Parliamentarian top class players – Lord Cowdrey of Tonbridge.

Almost from birth Cowdrey was destined for a cricketing career. Even his father – who bestowed the initials M. C. C. (Michael Colin) – could not, however, have anticipated his becoming the first Peer honoured exclusively for services to the great game.

Born in India in 1932, Colin Cowdrey's talents were quickly spotted at Tonbridge School by coach Ewart Astill. Youngest player to appear in a school match at Lord's, the 13-year-old scored 75 against Clifton although selected primarily for his leg spin bowling. Henceforth it has been a career as smooth and majestic as his style at the crease, with injury at some key moments the only hiccup. Blue and skipper of Oxford University 1952-54, he had already been capped for Kent (at only 18) in 1950. He played 402 matches for the county until retirement in 1976, captaining them for 14 seasons (1957-71) during which they won the County Championship.

The Cowdrey Test career was almost as lengthy – 1954 to 1975, with six visits to Australia. He was vice-captain in four but, to admitted disappointment, never led a tour there. In his 114 Tests he was, however, captain on 27 occasions (eight wins; four defeats), finishing with an average of 44.06 with 22 centuries. A splendidly safe fielder, mainly at slip, his 120 catches beat the then Hammond Test record for a non wicketkeeper.

Several of Cowdrey's international performances are part of cricketing history. In only his fifth Test innings, he scored 102 out of 191 against Australia in a match England won with the famous 7-27 burst from Frank Tyson. His 154 against West India at Birmingham in 1957 (in a 411 stand with his friend Peter May) is in many ways even more legendary. Together they "did for" Sonny Ramadhin as a Test bowler. Again in Australia (1962-63) he made his highest score (307 v South Australia) but although he exceeded 1000 runs in a home season 21 times, he reached 2,000 only twice.

Cowdrey's county career had several peaks – notably Kent winning a championship in their centenary year (1970). It was he who, with Les Ames as Manager, forged the successful Kent teams of the 1970s. And there was an almost magical finale. Those privileged to see him score 151 not out against the 1975 Australians at Canterbury to steer Kent to a famous victory, with a grimacing Ian Chappell as their captain, will never forget the power and style. For the record his first-class career saw an average of 42.89 in 692 matches with 107 centuries and 638 catches. The occasional leg spin captured 65 wickets at 51.21 apiece.

Last Men In

So much for the playing record but service to cricket more generally has continued apace. President of MCC in their bicentenary year (1986), he was then chairman of the International Cricket Conference 1989-93 – momentous years which saw South Africa quickly back into the Test match fold. Finally his creation as a Conservative Life Peer in 1997 – Lord Cowdrey of Tonbridge – where he has raised the sporting banner frequently in the Upper House. One recalls especially a debate he initiated in June 1999 when he rang out a 'clarion call' for higher standards of sportsmanship, fair play and, yes, more fun in British sport. Batting with him, predictably, that afternoon in this 'other Lords' were Charles Williams and David Sheppard.

David Sheppard's contribution to sport also remains unfinished but his life story to date is equal to Colin Cowdrey in its dedication and skill.

Another talented youngster, he also made his first-class debut, for Sussex in 1947, whilst still at Sherborne. Thence to Cambridge where he scored a century (against Sussex!) in his first innings. Later that same 1950 season, at only 21, he shared an opening stand of 343 with John Dewes against the West Indian tourists, with two other promising youngsters, Ramadhin and Valentine, amongst their bowlers. Sheppard scored 227 in 63½ hours at the crease for a Cambridge total of 594-4. It was a good wicket. The West Indies replied with 730-3 – Weekes 304 not out.

Then quickly into Test cricket at The Oval. No century start this time but Sheppard's 29 runs in the England second innings was the highest score as the West Indians went to an innings victory. Ramadhin got him in the first innings, Valentine in the second.

A blue in all three years at Cambridge (1950-52) and captain in the last, David Sheppard still holds several Oxbridge all-time records – most runs and centuries in a season (1,581 in 1952 with 7 hundreds) and 14 centuries overall.

Nor must we ignore his records for Sussex. As captain in 1953 he took them from 13th to 2nd place in the championship, equalling their highest-ever position. This was Sheppard's final full season of first-class cricket, although there were many comebacks. The church career began to take over after he was ordained in 1955, but not before he had captained England twice in the 1954 series against Pakistan (1 win, 1 draw) as a stand-in for the sick Len Hutton.

Later The Revd Sheppard took a sabbatical from his job as warden of the Mayflower Family Centre to make a second tour of Australia and New Zealand (1962-63). He is therefore the only ordained minister to play Test cricket. That career then closed, as had his county record a year earlier, leaving career figures of 22 Tests with 3 centuries at an average of 37.80 and a first-class total of 15,838 runs in 230 matches at 43.51. There were some splendid close catches in his tally of 195.

David Sheppard's ecclesiastical following took him from Bishop Suffragan of Woolwich (1969-75) to Bishop of Liverpool (1975-97). The Life Peerage – for Labour – came in 1998. He had, of course, already made his mark in the Lords previously from the Bishops' Bench.

Lords Williams, Cowdrey and Sheppard. A fine trio to end this Parliamentary cricketing tale. They always ran well together, and whenever the great game is debated there, they still do.

Twelfth Men

THERE ARE those who would like to have gone in at number ten and had to settle for number 11, and there are many who would have liked the chance to have gone in anywhere. It now seems highly unlikely that Sir Robert Atkins, despite being a Sports Minister, an MP for 18 years and now an MEP, will get a chance to bowl his off-breaks either for Middlesex or Lancashire (although there are great expectations for his son James). In spite of being pictured on the front of a cricket magazine going out to bat with Bob Hawke of Australia, former Prime Minister John Major will not, it is certain, open the Surrey innings with Alec Stewart. He has settled happily for Presidency of the County in succession to other politicians of repute such as Lord (Robert) Carr.

Sir Nicholas Scott can claim that his wife is the great grand-daughter of the famous Lord Hawke, but in spite of his fine performances for Lords and Commons Cricket, the former MP for Chelsea is unlikely to force his way into the Yorkshire side on the strength of this tenuous relationship. Baron Rippon of Hexham had a better claim in that his father played 102 matches for Somerset between 1914 and 1937 and hit six centuries as an opening batsman. His uncle also played in the Somerset side, and Arthur and Albert Rippon are among a very few number of twin brothers who have appeared together in first-class cricket.

Politics, of course, once cost Ted Dexter the England captaincy. Dexter, later to be one of England's supremos, first played Test cricket in 1958 and was sent out to Australia the following winter to boost a sagging England side. A batsman of regal splendour, authority and tremendous power, he was capable of dealing with the quickest of bowling in an imperious manner. He also bowled somewhat erratic, but often effective, medium pace.

He captained England in Pakistan and India, 1961-62, and led the side from then until the end of 1964, with the exception of one Test against Pakistan in 1962 when Colin Cowdrey was on trial. He missed the tour of India, 1963-64, but captained against Australia in 1964. The following winter, England were due to go to South Africa, with Dexter expected to lead the side, but it was announced he was to stand as Conservative Candidate against Jim Callaghan, the future Labour Prime Minister, in South East Cardiff in the General Election in October 1964. A place was kept open for him, and when, as was generally expected, he was beaten by Callaghan, he duly joined the squad.

Dexter's predecessor as captain of Sussex, Robin Marlar, would be very much at home in Parliament. A fine off-spinner who twice dismissed Charles Williams in the Varsity match of 1953, and a vigorous captain who suffered neither fools nor tedium gladly, Marlar has had a varied and highly successful career outside cricket. Briefly a master at Eton and Librarian at Arundel, he has run his own business in marketing, personnel and public relations with a refreshing dynamism. As cricket correspondent for the *Sunday Times*, he continues to offer views which are consistently provocative and uncompromising.

In 1959, he contested Bolsover for the Conservatives; and three years later, he was the Conservative Candidate in the Leicester North East by-election. Ever forceful, he fought in the Newbury by-election of 1993 as The Referendum Candidate demanding the right of the individual to be heard on the Maastricht Treaty. Should Marlar ever enter Parliament, the whips will have a task on their hands.

There is always the possibility that a seat in the House of Commons will tame a man, although there is not too much evidence of this. In his biography of Charles Stewart Parnell, R. Parry O'Brien would suggest otherwise:

'Parnell's favourite pastime was cricket. He became captain of the Wicklow XI, and threw himself with zest into the game. A strict disciplinarian, always bent on victory, and ever ready to take advantage of every chance (which the rules allowed) to outwit his opponents, reserved, uncompromising, self-willed, he was obeyed and trusted rather than courted or liked.

'Before Mr Parnell entered politics, says one local figure, "he was pretty well known in the province of Leinster in the commendable character of cricketer. We considered him ill-tempered and a little hard in his conduct of that pastime. For example, when the next bat was not up to time, Mr Parnell, as captain of the fielders, used to claim a wicket. Of course he was within his rights in doing so but it was anything but relished in a country where the game is never played on the assumption that this rule will be enforced.

"In order to win a victory he did not hesitate to take advantage of the strict letter of the law. On one occasion a match was arranged between Wicklow team and an XI of the Phoenix Club, to be played on the ground of the latter in Phoenix Park. Mr Parnell's men, with great trouble and inconvenience, many of them having to take long drives in the early morning, assembled on the ground. A dispute occurred between Mr Parnell and the captain of the Phoenix team. The Wicklow men wished their own captain to give in, and let the match proceed. Mr Parnell was stubborn, and, rather than give up his point, marched his growling XI back. That must have been a pleasant party so returning without their expected day's amusement, but the captain did not care. In later years, Mr Parnell used to use the Irish party much as he used the Wicklow XI."'

Parnell's cricket, of course, was not first-class, and he might well have met his match when faced by a side led by Grace, Wooller, Jardine or Marlar.

The problem with many sportsmen, and politicians, is that so multifarious are their talents that virtues which bring success in one aspect of their lives hinder advance in others. Not that much hindered C. B. Fry's progress in any direction, but he was once considered as a Labour candidate, stood as a Liberal and spoke on behalf of a Conservative when he was really an Independent.

Before his 22nd birthday, Charles Burgess Fry had been honoured by a Spy cartoon in *Vanity Fair*. It was entitled 'Oxford Athletics' and depicted a young man resembling a Greek god anticipating immediate action. The text which accompanied the drawing spoke of Fry as 'an enterprising boy who may always be relied upon to do as well as he is expected to do. He is generally ready for fun being full of all the strongest instincts of a young barbarian at play.'

He was, at that time – April 1894 – in his third year at Wadham College, Oxford. He had established a world record in the long jump which was to stand for 21 years and had taken a First Class in Classical Moderations. He had been president of the Athletic Club and captain of the soccer side. He was also captain of cricket, and, within three months of his appearance in *Vanity Fair*, he would score a century in the Varsity match in leading his side to victory over Cambridge. He would also be chosen to play rugby against Cambridge only to be denied that further blue because of injury. He also had the reputation to be able and willing to speak upon anything. The problem was, in fact, how to stop him.

Shortly after coming down from Oxford, he toured South Africa with Lord Hawke's side and played in his first two Test matches. Although often asked, he was never again available to tour. Among Fry's friends and contemporaries at Wadham were John Simon and F. E. Smith, later Earl of Birkenhead, both of whom were to become distinguished politicians, but Fry's first means of earning a living were restricted to teaching and journalism. As a sportsman, he continued to prosper.

He was capped for England against Ireland at soccer in 1901, and the following year played at right-back for Southampton against Sheffield

United in the FA Cup Final. In 1901, he hit six centuries in successive innings and amassed 3,147 runs, average 78.67, in the season. This was one of five seasons in his career, which lasted until 1921, when he averaged above 70.

Fry was an integral part of F. S. Jackson's successful side in 1905 and hit 144 in the final Test against the Australians. He himself led England in the Triangular Tournament in 1912, and under him England won four and drew two Tests. He had captained Sussex from 1904 to 1908 after which he moved to Hampshire where he had established his training ship *Mercury*.

He had started his magazine in 1904, written with intelligence and perception on cricket, and now, as he gave his full attention to *Mercury*, he was asked whether he would consider standing for Parliament. He was interested and nominated Oxford City as the constituency he would most like to contest, but then he felt he should defer his political career in favour of his other interests.

Fry's political ambitions surfaced at the end of the First World War when, through his friend Ranjitsinhji, he became deeply involved in the affairs of the League of Nations. In 1919, attending a League meeting at Chichester, he made an impromptu speech on the worth of the organisation. Labour activists asked him to stand as their candidate for Horsham and Worthing, but after he had spoken at another meeting they told him that he was a Liberal and found another to fight the seat.

Three years later, there were suggestions that he should represent the combined Labour and Liberal interests in the same constituency, but then he was offered the attractive proposition of being the Liberal Candidate at Brighton where two members were returned. He had the backing of the Liberal hierarchy and of such celebrities as Ranjitsinhji and the singer Clara Butt (Fry always numbered many friends in the arts), but there was a certain innocence in his campaigning in comparison to his Tory opponents.

He polled 22,059 votes, a remarkable achievement, but finished 4,785 short of the second Conservative. In the previous election, the Conservatives had beaten their Labour opponents by almost 24,000 votes.

General Elections were coming thick and fast at this period in British history, and at the end of 1923, amid much celebration, C. B. Fry was adopted as the Liberal Candidate for the Banbury Division of Oxfordshire. There was great optimism in the Liberal camp that Fry would win, for it was believed that the Labour candidate, Captain Bennett, who had polled 6,463 votes a year earlier, would not be standing and that Fry would take most of his votes thus ousting the Tory, Major Edmondson. At the last moment, Captain Bennett announced that he would defy doctor's orders and run again. The progressive vote was split, and Edmondson was returned with a majority of 219 votes over Fry.

There was to be yet another chance for Fry, for Frank Gray, who had won Oxford for the Liberals that same election, was disqualified on account of financial irregularities. Gray himself was blameless, but he could not stand again, and Fry replaced him at the by-election. Gray had won in a straight fight with the Conservative, but Fry was again to suffer from the intervention of a Labour candidate. All three candidates were blues. On that basis alone, Fry with 12 would have won but the progressive vote was split and he lost by 1,842 votes.

It is easy to blame the intervention of Labour for Fry's two defeats in Oxfordshire, but, for all his exuberance, intelligence and oratory, Charles Fry was a naive campaigner, not always conversant with the problems of the day. His response to a lady elector who was concerned with land for the 'sacred pheasant' was direct but unlikely to be persuasive. "Madam, when a pheasant is on the wing and I have a gun in my hand, I find it difficult to treat it as a sacred bird." Another effort went down better. Asked why unemployment was so low in France, he replied: "I have no idea – no idea whatsoever. Bowled me middle stump – neck and crop. By the way, what does neck and crop mean?"

There were rumours later that Fry might fight Horncastle in 1926 for the Liberals, and even Oxford City again, but Fry's devotion to free enterprise saw him speaking on behalf of the Conservative candidate at the Wavertree by-election in Liverpool in the mid-1930s.

Fry's politics were not restricted to the domestic. He attended three assemblies of the League of Nations with Ranjitsinhji for whom he often wrote speeches. It was during the first assembly in 1920 that Fry was approached to become King of Albania. Whether this was a genuine approach or, as was later suggested, a joke played by Ranjitsinhji on his friend, we shall never know, but it has that touch of the exotic that is consistent with Fry's life.

As Neville Cardus remarked in his autobiography, Fry could have been so many things. 'I have been told that if Fry had not squandered his talents on games and pursuits diverse and sometimes mutually exclusive, he might have distinguished himself in (1) politics, (2) the theatre, (3) the law, (4) literature. For my part I think there are politicians and KC's enough; there has only been one C. B. Fry.'

Before we become too convinced that, by some cruelty of fate, the House of Commons was denied a flawless and varied talent the like of which has never been equalled, let us reflect upon E. M. Wellings' account of the tale told to him by Percy Chapman.

'It is human nature to be amused when the great slip. From Percy Chapman I heard of his first sight of Fry at a country house game. Percy was taken along as a spectator and Fry was a player. The pavilion enclosure was surrounded by a very low white fence. Fry appeared carrying a tea tray for the ladies. He hurdled the low white fence, cut it too fine and nose-dived, tea tray and all. "My first sight of the great athlete," Percy commented.'

Perhaps it was all too symbolic of Fry's political aspirations, but there was something indestructible in the man. Unable to fight in the First World War because of his work with *Mercury*, he was too old for the Second. Undeterred, in 1942, at the age of 70, he volunteered to go down the mines as a Bevin Boy.

Percy Fender might well have played a prominent part in this narrative. Three times he was asked to stand as a Conservative candidate, and three times he rejected the offer. There was a fourth approach from a Kent constituency when he might have accepted, but the president of the local association was Lord Harris. He vetoed the choice of Fender. Fender had crossed swords with Harris on several occasions and had even written indiscreetly about his lordship. Harris was too powerful a man to offend in this way.

A colourful, controversial figure, Fender was always in the news for his social activities, and although he was an outstanding captain of Surrey, he never led England. His political career was limited to two terms as Conservative Member of the London County Council for the Norwood Division of Lambeth, 1952 to 1958.

Fender began his career with Sussex, but he played for Surrey from 1914 until 1935. His career at The Oval did not coincide with that of George Ricketts or John Raphael. Indeed, Ricketts' first-class career was contained in one season, 1887, when he was in Oxford's victorious team against Cambridge. He had earned his blue on the strength of an innings of 92 in 90 minutes, including 13 fours, against a strong Lancashire side, and he later played three times for Surrey, an equally strong side, but with little success.

A fine all-round sportsman, Ricketts stood six feet five inches and was an immensely powerful batsman as well as a good fielder. He went with Lord Hawke's side to North America in 1891 and hit 71 not out in the last match of the tour, against Eastern Ontario, but his first-class career was limited to 13 matches in 1887. He served on the MCC Committee, but, as with so many other cricketing politicians, the legal profession claimed most of his time. He was Recorder of Portsmouth and a Bencher of the Inner Temple.

In 1909, he married the widow of his Oxford team-mate Edward Buckland, and the next year he twice contested Winchester, where he had gone to school, for the Liberal cause. In both the January and the December he was unsuccessful, and that seems to have blunted his political aspirations.

Like Ricketts, John Raphael was an unsuccessful Liberal candidate. He unsuccessfully fought a by-election at Croydon and his early death ended what might have been a fine political career in the years immediately after the First World War.

As a schoolboy at Merchant Taylor, Raphael had a brilliant record, being in the XI for four years, scoring hugely and taking many wickets.

He seemed set for an outstanding career at Oxford, having already made his first-class debut for London County in 1901. But after a promising Freshmen's Match in 1902, his form completely deserted him, and he did not appear in a first-class match. It seemed that his career at Oxford in 1903 would follow the same pattern as it had traced in his first season, but he was appearing for Surrey. He did well for Surrey against his university and then played for Oxford against Sussex, hitting 65 while all around him fell. On the strength of this, William Findlay gave Raphael the last place in the side to meet Cambridge. Raphael opened and was ninth out. He hit 130 when the next highest score was 21.

He was now appearing regularly for Surrey and was one of five amateurs to captain the county in the messy season of 1904. He was invited to lead the side in 1905 after the season at Oxford, but, as we noted earlier, Lord Dalmeny, later Lord Rosebery, took over.

In 1905, Raphael came close to equalling William Yardley's record of two centuries in Varsity matches, but he was bowled by an unstoppable ball from Napier when he was on 99. This was his last Varsity match as he now found he had less and less time to assist Surrey.

A wonderful all-round sportsman, he won blues for swimming, water polo and rugby, a sport in which he was one of the outstanding players of his generation winning nine caps for England as a back between 1902 and 1906. His was an exceptional individual talent, and he scored a try in three of his four Varsity matches.

On the Raphael family estate at Shenley in Hertfordshire, a cricket ground was laid out to the exact dimensions of The Oval, and here John Raphael played and practised. Born in Belgium in 1882, he was to die in Belgium in 1917. The ground at Shenley was neglected by a saddened family, and in 1927, the estate was bought by the Middlesex County Council, and for the next decade, Radlett Cricket Club played at Shenley.

The home had become a mental hospital, but when the hospital was closed the Shenley Park was developed by a Trust. In 1993, the ground, restored and beautiful, was reopened, and under the guidance of the former Middlesex and England cricketer Eric Russell, was until recently on its way to becoming a centre of excellence. Perhaps the memory and name of a young man who never quite fulfilled himself as cricketer or politician will be evoked.

There were cricketers who found that even if they did not seek politics, they were touched by the House of Commons or the House of Lords somehow. For example, sports writer Charles Bray was for a while a lobby correspondent. He played 95 games for Essex, averaging 24, and indeed captained them when Holmes and Sutcliffe put on their famous 555 opening stand at Leyton, but he did not perform on the floor of the House itself.

For the solid, long-serving Kent batsman James Seymour, the House of Lords was the ultimate salvation. He took his benefit in the match against Hampshire at Canterbury in 1920. There were attempts to tax the benefit, and this was used as a test court case which went as far as the House of Lords where it was established that it was the right of the cricket benefit, unless guaranteed by contract, to be free from tax. There are very many first-class cricketers who have been grateful to Seymour and the House of Lords in the 70 odd years since that judgement. Not surprisingly Lord Harris had a hand in it.

If politics affects all our lives, cricket has been important in the lives of many politicians. Perhaps we should leave the last word to an historian, the late E. P. Thompson. One of his great heroes was Nehru to whom he was introduced as a child. What did Nehru say to the boy, the future socialist historian? 'He showed me how to hold my cricket bat.'

Index

Index

Peel, Robert, Sir 13, 24, 28, 42, 92
Perceval, Spencer 17
Pevensey, Henry North Holroyd 39, 40, 41
Pitt, William 17, 58
Ponsonby, Frederick 33
Ponsonby, Hon H. 27
Ponsonby, Spencer Cecil Brabazon 35
Portland, Lord 17
Priestley, Sir Arthur 93, 94
Proctor 9
Prothero, Rowland Edmund 99, 100
Queen Elizabeth 10
Queen Victoria 56, 62
Ranjitsinhji, Prince 8, 56, 94, 119, 120, 122, 123, 179, 181
Raphael, John 136, 137, 182, 183
Rees-Davies, William Rupert 160, 161, 162
Reid, Robert Threshie 66, 67, 68
Remnant, Peter 155, 156, 159
Remnant, Robert John 155
Reynolds, Joshua 22, 168
Rhodes, Wilfred 110, 134
Richardson, H. A. 61
Richardson, John Maunsell 76, 77, 78, 79, 80
Ricketts, George 182
Rimbault, G. A. 159
Ring, George 21
Ring, John 24
Rippon, Albert 175
Rippon, Arthur 175
Rippon, Barron 175
Robins, Walter 126, 150

Robinson, Sir Benjamin 56
Roller 92
Rosebery, Earl of 67, 80, 136, 137, 138, 151, 183
Rothermere, Lord 165
Round, James 60, 62, 72
Russell, Charles, Lord 36
Russell, Eric 184
Russell, John, Lord 13, 15, 36, 42, 70
Sackville, John Frederick 21
Salisbury, Marquis of 43, 44, 51, 55, 62
Sanderson, Lancelot 94, 96, 97
Scott, Sir Nicholas 8, 86, 175
Seymour, G.A. 12
Seymour, James 184
Shaw, Alfred 39, 40
Sheppard, David 173, 174
Sidebottom, Alexander 33
Silkin, Sam 159, 160
Simon, John 178
Smith, C. A. 37
Smith, F. E. 178
Smith, J. K. 170, 171
Smith, W. H. 55
Smith-Barry, Arthur Hugh 60, 62
Smyth, Jackie MP 9, 159
Smyth, John, Brigadier 159
Sobers 9
St Albans, Fifth Duke of 19
Standing, Percy Cross 90, 91, 93
Stanhope, Rt Hon Edward 49, 50, 51
Stanley, Lord 24
Stanyforth, R. T. 150
Stephenson, J. W. A. 161
Stewart, Alec 175

Index